On Resilience:
Stories of Climate Adaptation
Across Washington's
Landscapes

On Resilience: Stories of Climate Adaptation Across Washington's Landscapes
by Harriet Morgan and Lindsay Senechal
with Writing the Land® Poets

Foreword by Thor Hanson
Preface by CMarie Fuhrman
Poems by Writing the Land® Poets

Published by NatureCulture®
www.nature-culture.net ~ www.writingtheland.org

ISBN: 978-1-960293-19-0
First Edition

Cover Artwork: Jill Pelto
www.jillpelto.com

Cover design: Christopher Gendron
Interior book design: Lis McLoughlin

On Resilience:
Stories of Climate Adaptation Across Washington's Landscapes

by Harriet Morgan and Lindsay Senechal,
Washington Department of Fish and Wildlife

with Writing the Land® Poets

Foreword by Thor Hanson
Preface by CMarie Fuhrman

Published by
NatureCulture
Northfield, MA

Acknowledgments

This project would not have been possible without the expertise and generous participation of WDFW's Wildlife Area Managers and Water Access Managers. Their willingness to connect with poets, share insights on local management challenges, and, in some cases, provide on-the-ground tours of the landscapes they work in enriched this project immensely.

A special thank you to Jill Pelto (cover art) and Simone Des Roches (chapter illustrations), whose creativity and talent brought Washington's landscapes and wildlife to life in ways that words alone cannot. Through intricate details and scale, their work invites the reader to envision a future where people and nature thrive in a changing climate.

Wildlife Area	Wildlife Manager Support
North Olympic Wildlife Area	Katie Laushman
Olympic Wildlife Area	Nick Bechtold
Skagit Wildlife Area	Greg Meis
Scatter Creek Wildlife Area	Bill Kronland
Mount Saint Helens Wildlife Area	Zach Breitenstein
Shillapoo Wildlife Area	Zach Breitenstein
Sinlahekin Wildlife Area	Nathan Wehmeyer
Scotch Creek Wildlife Area	Bryan Dupont
Cowlitz Wildlife Area	Richard Vanderlip
L.T. Murray Wildlife Area	Shawn Morrison
Wenas Wildlife Area	Melinda Gray
Klickitat Wildlife Area	Melinda Gray
Swanson Lakes Wildlife Area	Mike Finch
Sunnyside-Snake River Wildlife Area	Pat Kaelber
Methow Wildlife Area	Alex Repp
W.T. Wooten Wildlife Area	Kari Dingman
Asotin Creek Wildlife Area	Bob Dice

Acknowledging the Indigenous People of the Pacific Northwest

Since time immemorial, Indigenous People have lived in the Pacific Northwest and hunted, fished, and gathered natural resources, traditional foods, and medicinal plants to support their diverse cultures. They were the original occupants and stewards of this land that all Washingtonians enjoy today. The very survival of the Pacific Northwest Tribes is a testament to their resilience in the face of what they have endured and continue to endure throughout generations on this landscape. Through many historical encounters—including massacres, renunciation of religious freedom, systemic racism, cultural assimilation of Native children through institutional residential schools, and the fight for their inherent rights and liberties—they have prevailed. Throughout this painful history brought by colonization, abrogated treaties, infringement of civil rights, and the salmon protests of the 1960s, the Northwest Tribes and the Washington Department of Fish and Wildlife (WDFW) have founded a commitment of respect, unity, and alliance informed by the realities of the past. Today, tribal governments and WDFW work collaboratively to conserve and manage aquatic and terrestrial resources statewide and practice sound science to guide management decisions. Together, the Tribes and WDFW work to ensure the sustainability of fish, wildlife, ecosystems, and culture for the next seven generations and beyond.

Disclaimer

A Letter from the Director of the Washington Department of Fish and Wildlife

At the Washington Department of Fish and Wildlife, we are entrusted with the vital responsibility of being the principal steward of Washington's fish and wildlife resources. Our mission is to preserve, protect, and perpetuate fish, wildlife, and ecosystems while providing sustainable fish and wildlife recreational and commercial opportunities. With over 1 million acres of public land under our stewardship, we work to maintain the delicate balance between thriving wildlife and vibrant communities, ensuring these resources remain resilient and accessible for generations to come.

Yet, the climate is changing, reshaping the landscapes we manage and the assumptions that have guided our work. Rising temperatures, shrinking snowpack, more frequent wildfires, and shifting water availability are impacting the ecosystems that sustain us all. These challenges demand innovation, adaptability, and a commitment to rethinking how we approach conservation in a world where the old 'normal' no longer applies. Grounded in science and guided by expert judgment, we are adjusting our natural resource management strategies in response to the ongoing and projected impacts of climate change. We strive to honor the intangible and immeasurable qualities of the land: its stories, its resilience, and its capacity to sustain both nature and humanity—physically, emotionally, and culturally.

No matter how daunting the future may seem, it isn't written yet. That means we have a choice. Climate change is complex and difficult, but every day brings us the chance to shape the future we want. This is a future we can only create through thoughtful action, guided by science, inspired by connection, and rooted in our shared commitment and responsibility to Washington's fish, wildlife, and landscapes.

This anthology reflects that shared responsibility and possibility. It tells the story of how WDFW is adapting our natural resource practices to meet the realities of a changing climate and celebrates the resilience we see in the species and landscapes of Washington. It also weaves together the threads of poetry and purpose, offering a collection of verses that capture the deep connections between people, nature, and place.

Each poem is a call to remember what is at stake and what is possible. Hope, rooted in reality, challenges us to imagine a future where both people and nature thrive in the face of a changing climate.

As you read, I invite you to consider the challenges and opportunities ahead, to reflect on what is possible when we work together, and to find inspiration in the beauty and resilience of Washington's landscapes. Together, let us forge that path of progress which tempers innovation with reverence, for a bright tomorrow where our state's habitats and species not only survive but thrive.

Onward,

Kelly Susewind, Director
Washington Department of Fish and Wildlife

Foreword: On Resilience

In January, earth tones dominate the view from my office window. I look out across a thicket of umber willow whips and berry canes, winter-bare, and twined through with the lighter shades of hardhack, the ruddy twigs of rose, and the gray-brown branches of a crabapple. So why was I seeing pink? I blinked and looked again, but it was still there, an unmistakable scattering of springtime brightness. Tricked by a week of unseasonable warmth, the salmonberries had begun to bloom.

This, I knew with a pang, meant far more than a jarring moment. Freezing weather would soon return, crisping the blossoms and triggering a long cascade of want: bumblebees and hummingbirds deprived of nectar, thrushes deprived of fruit, and the plants themselves deprived of a means to disperse their seeds. But I also knew that nature is not defenseless. A quick survey of the yard reassured me that many other salmonberry canes had not been fooled; their flowers remained safely tucked inside unopened buds. Gooseberries, twinberries, and currants also seemed unaffected. Apparently, one false spring would not be enough to unravel the real thing. But of course the number of false springs is on the rise, and every one exacts a cost.

Look out from any window in Washington state and you're likely to see some version of this same story playing out. Seasons are shifting as the planet warms, but so are shorelines and treelines, and for many species, the very boundaries of the ranges they inhabit. Unpredictable conditions and upended relationships make surprises a commonplace, some as subtle as an early flower, others as forceful as fire or flood. The results can be unsettling, particularly for those who live close to the land, and for those tasked with caring for it. But there are also examples of species and systems that seem to thrive on change, or at least hold their own, and for many others the challenges can be mitigated. Understanding why, and how, are vital steps toward resilience.

In the context of such upheaval, this volume is a timely and thoughtful response. It was crafted by scientists and land managers in partnership with poets and artists, a wise pairing, because changes to the land are also a matter of heart. In these pages you will find descriptions of habitats and climate adaptations for natural areas all across the state, alongside verses and images that give those landscapes voice. Together, they link what we know and predict with what we feel. That's a helpful framework for a world in flux, because as the land changes, so do the stories we tell.

As a biologist and a writer, I found this book filled with fresh insights into familiar creatures and settings, much like a fine walk in nature. I also found myself eager to explore the many places it describes, and that impulse is a lesson in itself, a reminder to go outside observe, and take action. There is a lot to learn from wild things in wild places. When the climate changes, they respond in every way they can. So must we all.

—Thor Hanson
San Juan Island

Preface: Poets Connect Us to the Land

The earth is so glad you are here.

I like to begin classes and readings in this way, especially when we are celebrating, investigating, or learning about this landscape we call home. Like so many other beings, we depend on it.

I often follow by acknowledging the claim: that while the earth needs its birds, ants, and cyanobacteria, it would be better off without humans. A claim I strongly disagree with.

My ancestors, the ancestors of many Native poets in these pages, and likely those somewhere in your own lineage, celebrated this land with song and ceremony, expressing a deep and reciprocal relationship with the natural world. Here, in the region now called Washington, more broadly Cascadia, but originally known by many other names, the language, culture, and lifeways were born from, not merely influenced by, the land and its beings. In some traditions, the land and beings created the people. In most tribes, they taught us their names and how to live through stories and songs, crafting a language born from listening closely to the land and her beings.

In a gift community, one that understands reciprocity, gratitude is inherent. Before colonization, the landscape was awakened with ceremony by people offering a dawn chorus like the birds, and an evening song like the coyote. There were dances for Bear, and weeks-long celebrations for the return of Salmon. More importantly, among all the beings who called this area home, there was relationship. There was the understanding that our relatives not only walked on two legs, but also slithered, flooded, and flew. Community extended beyond the firelight of humans; family was not limited to those who looked like us.

Among many Native people, this understanding remains true today.

I have celebrated the return of Salmon with the Nimiipuu. I have remembered that every dip of my paddle into water is a prayer. And I know that Earth has eyes, and I strive to live in a way that would not bring shame to myself or my people for how I treat the more-than-human world.

As the partner of a fisheries biologist, I know this holds true for many others. They may wear titles like land manager, biologist, or range scientist, but their work is rooted in attention. To see, understand, and celebrate the natural world—to study—is a form of devotion, and devotion to the land, I believe, is our purpose on this planet. Praise. Celebration. Song. Dance. Stewardship. Devotion. This was and is our purpose. For those who claim we bring only harm, that beyond our capacity to perceive beauty, learn from her beings, and celebrate Earth and this region in all its diversity, complexity, nuance, and contradictions, we have done nothing but harm—I disagree.

We are about to be tested. Or, perhaps, my theory is about to be tested. We can, like the poets, the researchers and land managers, and the Native people who have lived on this land for nearly 20,000 years, nurture a mutually beneficial relationship with the Earth, directing our energy, creativity, witnessing, and celebration toward her beings. Or, we can succumb to the distractions of devices, divisive politics, and rampant consumerism, which pull us further from our purpose. Devotion is a breath away from love, and true love does not thrive on the loss and continual harm of another.

Lately, I have been asked what the role of the poet is in land stewardship. My answer is that the role of the poet who writes about beings and land is no different than the role of the poet who writes about anything else: to connect. To connect us to the rhythms of the land, to the cycles of reciprocity that mirror the turning seasons. To remind us that we are not separate from the web of life, but integral to it. Every poet in this collection is offering you their truth, bringing word from the oracle, celebrating and honoring the land with their gifts—gifts that are undeniably felt in the same way our own excitement is felt when we are recognized. In this act of connection, in this gift of language, we offer our gratitude, our celebration, our very being back to the land that sustains us, completing the circle of reciprocity.

Read these poems aloud. Read them outside, to the plant beings in your yard. Read them at rallies to protect the land. Send them to government officials. Staple them to fenceposts. Let them be your ceremony, your inspiration, your guide to living alongside the more-than-human world. And while you are at it, thank your local land steward, biologist, scientist, conservationist, and public lands employee. They flourish with your appreciation, too.

Our purpose, the very reason the Earth is glad we are here, is to celebrate, to make art, to love this planet—to love it to life, and to use that love to care for it—and to be guides, like these poets and land stewards, into this way of being. To fail in this is to fail not only our ancestors and predecessors, but to betray the very reason we exist on this planet, the home of all beings.

Kindly,
CMarie Fuhrman
author of *Salmon Weather: Writing From the Land of No Return*
and co-editor of *Cascadia Field Guide: Art, Ecology, and Poetry*

Photo opposite by CMarie Fuhrman

ON RESILIENCE:
STORIES OF CLIMATE ADAPTATION ACROSS WASHINGTON'S LANDSCAPES
TABLE OF CONTENTS

A map of Washington's nine ecoregions—geographically distinct areas shaped by climate, geology, and ecological characteristics. Each ecoregion has a dedicated chapter, exploring climate change impacts to these landscapes. The pins represent Department

Sinlahekin
Wildlife Area

Methow
Wildlife Area

Scotch Creek
Wildlife Area

Northern Rockies

Swanson Lakes
Wildlife Area

Swanson Lakes
Wildlife Area

Wenas
Wildlife Area

Columbia Plateau

Sunnyside-Snake River
Wildlife Area

W.T. Wooten
Wildlife Area

Asotin Creek
Wildlife Area

Blue
Mountains

of Fish and Wildlife's Wildlife Areas featured in the anthology, where management objectives, climate resilience efforts, and ecological significance are examined alongside poetry inspired by firsthand visits to these sites. Image credit: WDFW.

Washington Department of
FISH & WILDLIFE

INTRODUCTION
by Harriet Morgan

Introduction

Washington's landscapes are defined by incredible ecological diversity, spanning from the temperate rainforests of the Olympic Peninsula to the arid sagebrush of the Columbia Plateau. These ecosystems support a variety of fish, wildlife, and plant species, each uniquely adapted to local environmental conditions. The Washington Department of Fish and Wildlife (WDFW) is responsible for managing these resources in accordance with our mission: To preserve, protect, and perpetuate fish, wildlife, and ecosystems while providing sustainable fish and wildlife recreational and commercial opportunities.

Yet, Washington's landscapes are changing. Warming temperatures, sea-level rise, increasing flood risk, decreasing mountain snowpack, declining summer water availability, and increased wildfire potential are impacting ecosystems and the fish and wildlife that depend on them. Some of these climate impacts are readily observed—such as stream temperatures warming past the physiological limits of salmon, or shrubsteppe ecosystems transformed by wildfires fueled by invasive grasses. Other climate impacts are more subtle, but no less significant, such as mismatches between species' life cycle stages and food availability—for example, earlier flowering times due to a warming climate may no longer align with the activity periods of pollinators. To address these challenges, WDFW is adapting its approach to natural resource management to respond to both on-going and projected climate impacts.

The impacts of climate change are not solely ecological; they also challenge fundamental assumptions that guide natural resource management. For decades, WDFW's management decisions—on everything from fishing and hunting seasons to hatchery operations, lands stewardship, and habitat restoration—have been informed, in part, by long-standing assumptions of climate stability, relying on historical climate conditions as a guide for present and future management. However, the challenge is that these assumptions, which once provided a reliable foundation for decision-making, are increasingly misaligned with the realities of a changing climate. Recognizing these challenges, WDFW has begun a deliberate effort to daylight where these climate assumptions exist and create space to discuss how management strategies can be altered to account for projected changes.

This anthology serves three interconnected purposes: to document the ongoing and projected impacts of climate change on Washington's habitats and species, to examine how WDFW is adapting natural resource management practices to build resilience to climate change, and to honor the power of poetry in capturing the connections humans have with Washington's landscapes in a time of rapid human-driven change.

The structure of this anthology is organized around Washington's nine ecoregions—geographically distinct areas shaped by climate, geology, and ecological characteristics. Washington's ecoregions include the Coast Range, Puget Lowland, Willamette Valley, North Cascades, West Cascades, East Cascades, Columbia Plateau, Blue Mountains, and Northern Rockies. Climate change will affect each of these ecoregions in distinct ways, and we aim to capture these differences throughout the anthology's nine chapters, one dedicated for each ecoregion.

Each ecoregional chapter highlights one to four WDFW Wildlife Areas, examining their management objectives and providing place-based examples of how WDFW's natural resource management is building resilience to climate change.* Accompanying these management write-ups, each chapter also features poetry inspired by the Wildlife Areas in that ecoregion. Poets contributing to this anthology were assigned a specific Wildlife Area and visited the site to learn firsthand about its ecosystems, fish, wildlife, and plant communities, allowing them to reflect on the connections between land, climate, and management.

In addition to site-specific poetry, most chapters also include contributions from ecoregional poets—a group of Indigenous poets who were invited to write about any lands within their assigned ecoregion. These poems offer a broader perspective on place, history, and identity, illuminating the relationships between people, land, and climate. Northwest Tribal and Indigenous communities are at the forefront of climate adaptation, leading innovative and place-based strategies that strengthen ecosystem resilience and protect natural and cultural resources. These poems accompany the ecoregional profiles, centering Indigenous voices and deepening the conversation about climate resilience, resource management, and our collective responsibility to steward the landscapes we depend on.

---

*Management objectives and place-based examples are derived from WDFW Wildlife Area manager expertise and personal communication, WDFW's Wildlife Area Management Plans, and WDFW's climate report: *Preparing Washington Department of Fish and Wildlife for a Changing Climate: Assessing Risks and Opportunities for Action.*

COAST RANGE ECOREGION

Coast Range Ecoregion
Poet Misty Shipman

North Olympic Wildlife Area
Poet Victoria Pinheiro

Olympic Wildlife Area
Poet Carolyn Maddux

Coast Range Ecoregion

The Coast Range Ecoregion spans the temperate rainforests of the Olympic Mountains, stretching west to the shores of the Pacific Ocean and east to Hood Canal, encompassing a diverse array of habitats and species that call them home. Mature coniferous forests, dominated by Sitka spruce, Douglas fir, and western red cedar provide habitat for wildlife such as black-tailed deer, northern spotted owls, and marbled murrelets. Rivers and streams serve as habitat for anadromous fish species, particularly salmon, dependent upon intact riparian habitat and estuaries for spawning and rearing. River mouths transition to wetlands, estuaries, and beaches, which play vital roles in nutrient cycling and provide habitats for migratory shorebirds, shellfish populations, and marine mammals.

The Coast Range Ecoregion holds immense ecological value as a bridge between terrestrial and marine ecosystems, supporting species that depend on interconnected habitats. Bald eagles, for example, forage across forested uplands and coastal waters, while salmon link freshwater, terrestrial, and marine ecosystems through their life cycles. These habitats also provide essential services like flood regulation, water filtration, and carbon storage. However, the interconnectedness of this ecoregion makes it particularly vulnerable to disruption, highlighting the need for integrated conservation strategies to sustain its resilience.

Climate change is having profound effects on Washington's Coast Range Ecoregion. The Olympic Peninsula is experiencing sea-level rise, ocean acidification, heatwaves, and shifts in the region's hydrology – with a greater proportion of winter precipitation falling as rain instead of snow. Sea-level rise threatens to inundate low-lying habitats, erode the nearshore, and increase risk of flooding along the coastline.

The region's beaches, estuaries, and wetlands, which serve as critical habitats for numerous species, are especially vulnerable to these changes. Within the ecoregion, estuaries, such as Willapa Bay and the lower Columbia River, are vital for waterfowl, shorebirds, and juvenile fish, acting as both feeding grounds and migration corridors. Coastal wetlands, including the Grays Harbor National Wildlife Refuge, provide essential habitat for migratory birds traveling along the Pacific Flyway. As sea-levels rise, coastal habitats often try to move inland to adapt. However, this landward migration is often blocked by human-made structures like homes or buildings. When habitats can't move inland, they may shrink or disappear altogether, a challenge known as "coastal squeeze."

Climate change is also profoundly reshaping the hydrology of the Coast Range Ecoregion. Warmer winters are causing more precipitation to fall as rain instead of snow, reducing snowpack and leading to earlier river peak flows. These shifts increase the risk of winter flooding, which can scour streambeds, wash away salmon spawning nests, and raise sediment loads that degrade water quality. Summers, meanwhile, bring lower streamflows that reduce habitat connectivity, create barriers for migrating fish, and warm stream temperatures beyond the tolerance of cold-water species like salmon. Earlier peak flows further disrupt the timing of life cycles for migratory fish such as salmon and lamprey, creating mismatches between when fish migrate and when prey are available, intensifying stressors on already vulnerable populations.

Aerial view of a nearshore beach in Washington during a herring spawning event. The milky waters near the shoreline result from herring releasing milt, fertilizing eggs deposited on eelgrass and other nearshore vegetation. These spawning events play a crucial role in the marine ecosystem, providing essential forage for marine species. Photo credit: WDFW.

Song of Our Saints in the Sears Parking Lot
by Misty Shipman

The reservation dogs are barking on their leashes again
and it is Tuesday, a perpetual Tuesday of the mind
as I am imagining every wave that crashes against the
shore, every crab that scuttles sideways under this rock or that,
any rock will do. The oysters are burrowing into the ground,
defying whatever shovel that comes hunting, whatever child,
skirts hitched around her knees, that digs into the yielding dirt
to fill her bucket on these beaches that wash away
with each passing year, near the houses that sink into the cool
wet sand, and forget the memories of lovers laughing through the halls.

Isn't the body another kind of earth? Isn't the earth
another kind of body? Seed the wound. Confetti the party.
Blue smoke, or pink? Wake up.

They say a face is imprinted on the Shroud of Turin
like that's some kind of proof. Like the body is still entombed,
but you can't make me believe in nothing. I know a risen Lord
when I see one, and anyway, Jesus appeared to my aunt in her single-wide,
at the foot of her twin bed, brown-paneled walls and shag carpet
and the glow of that same blue moon at the window.
He said, "Don't be afraid," and I'm not.

Meanwhile the dogs are gnawing at the bones.
My stomach hurts again but that won't stop me.
I've known love as deep and wide as the Pacific Ocean.
I've seen the sky that goes on and on, past the horizon line
where colors melt into the sea. It's purple, and blue,
and red, and pink.

Nothing ever dies for real.

North Olympic Wildlife Area

The North Olympic Wildlife Area, located in Clallam County and Jefferson County, spans approximately 1,310 acres of managed lands throughout its units. It contains a mix of estuary, riverine, wetland, oak-prairie, and mixed forest habitats that support a diversity of wildlife, from big and small game species to songbirds, as well as native and federally endangered fish populations.

The wildlife area is managed for the protection and restoration of native plant communities and provides diverse opportunities for the public to access the landscape. Recreational opportunities are provided when it is compatible with the conservation of specific species and their habitats. Management of the wildlife area is dependent on partnerships with regional fisheries enhancement groups, tribes, and other crucial partnering organizations.

The Duckabush estuary, located along Hood Canal just south of Brinnon, Washington, is a vital habitat where the freshwater of the Duckabush River mixes with saltwater. This estuary provides critical habitat for fish, migratory birds, and other wildlife. Among its key roles is supporting the life cycle of salmon, offering juvenile fish a place to feed, rest, and transition to saltwater, increasing their chances of survival in the ocean. The estuary is home to several salmon and trout species, including Hood Canal summer chum, Puget Sound Chinook, and Puget Sound steelhead, all protected under the Endangered Species Act. However, like many estuaries throughout Puget Sound, the Duckabush has been altered, primarily through the construction of Highway 101 in 1934, which restricted natural water flow and disrupted habitat connectivity.

The Duckabush Restoration Project, led by WDFW in partnership with the U.S. Army Corps of Engineers, the Washington Department of Transportation, and the Hood Canal Salmon Enhancement Group, aims to address these environmental challenges. Plans include realigning Highway 101 upstream of its current location, removing old bridges and levees, and restoring historical estuary channels. The new elevated highway will include wider shoulders, better pedestrian and cyclist access, and improved runoff treatment to protect water quality. This redesign will reconnect tidal channels, reduce upstream flooding, and allow wildlife like elk to cross freely beneath the bridge.

Once completed, the restored Duckabush Estuary will support more productive habitats for fish, with newly colonized salt-tolerant vegetation helping to keep water temperatures cool and provide feeding and resting areas. The project is expected to contribute to the recovery of Hood Canal summer chum, a species nearing delisting thanks to ongoing conservation efforts. Additionally, healthier salmon populations will benefit Southern Resident killer whales and create better fishing opportunities for recreational anglers and tribes. The Duckabush restoration project is a rare opportunity to address long-standing environmental impacts and create lasting benefits for the ecosystem, the community, and beyond.

Aerial view of the Duckabush estuary restoration site, looking north. Highway 101 is visible in the distance, marking the location of the proposed Duckabush restoration project. This project will reconnect the estuary with natural tidal and riverine processes by modifying the highway infrastructure, improving habitat for fish and wildlife while enhancing ecosystem resilience. Photo credit: John Gussman.

Restoring estuaries is a crucial strategy for helping ecosystems and communities adapt to the challenges of climate change. Healthy estuaries serve as natural buffers against sea-level rise and storm surges, reducing the risk of flooding and erosion for communities. By re-establishing wetlands and other estuarine habitats, restoration projects create essential refuges and migration corridors for wildlife, enabling species to adapt to shifting conditions caused by a warming climate. Additionally, estuaries play a critical role in regulating local temperatures by cooling and shading surrounding waters, mitigating thermal stress on aquatic life. Estuary restoration increases ecological function, strengthens natural coastal defenses, and increases resilience to climate-driven disturbances, making it a critical strategy for long-term ecosystem resilience.

View from the Duckabush estuary looking northwest toward the Olympic Mountains. Photo credit: Harriet Morgan.

Place of the crooked waters
by Victoria Pinheiro

When they lift the road from the earth,
two ropes of swift-water will unravel into
threads of runnel and swale,
spreading through seablite and salt grass
in an exhale held for seventy years.
The river rocks, once swept clean,
will green with algae
and insects will flit among the
little salmon in the slow-water,
who skitter from shadow to shadow
in the brackish murk.
It takes seasons and work to forget urgency,
but the river will learn to rest again.

Olympic Wildlife Area

The Olympic Wildlife Area, part of the Olympic-Willapa Hills Wildlife Area complex, is managed by WDFW to conserve critical habitats, support diverse wildlife, and enhance landscape resilience. Spanning multiple parcels across Grays Harbor and Clallam Counties, the area is centered around the Wishkah River valley and focuses on providing winter forage for Roosevelt elk. By maintaining forage areas, WDFW helps reduce grazing pressure on nearby agricultural lands, helping to minimize conflicts between wildlife and private landowners. The area's riparian zones, upland meadows, and forested wetlands support a variety of species while also improving water retention, soil stability, and climate resilience of the landscape.

The Olympic Wildlife Area spans 40.7 acres along the Bogachiel River, approximately 5 miles south of Forks, Washington. Acquired in 1998 through a land donation, this unit serves as critical winter forage habitat for elk. By providing sufficient forage, the unit helps reduce elk reliance on private lands during the winter months, mitigating conflicts with agricultural and residential activities in the surrounding areas.

A hiker walks through a tree-lined, mowed field in a Wynoochee Mitigation Unit parcel, part of the Olympic Wildlife Area managed by WDFW to provide winter forage for Roosevelt elk and support habitat conservation. Photo credit: WDFW.

In addition to supporting elk populations, the Olympic Wildlife Area plays a vital role in conserving riparian habitat along the Bogachiel River. These riparian zones support water retention and stabilize riverbanks, helping to regulate streamflow and increasing aquatic habitat quality. WDFW has prioritized maintaining healthy vegetation along streambanks, including black cottonwood, alder, and native shrubs, which provide shade to the river, which is especially important as stream temperatures are projected to increase in Washington due to warming air temperatures and decreasing summer streamflows, putting additional stress on cold-water fish species. Temperature-sensitive fish such as coho, Chinook, chum salmon, and cutthroat trout depend on cool, oxygen-rich water for survival. As water temperatures rise, oxygen availability decreases, increasing stress on fish populations and reducing their ability to successfully spawn and rear. By maintaining dense root structures along streambanks, these plants also reduce sediment erosion, which helps keep the water clear and prevents fine sediments from smothering salmon eggs.

The Olympic Wildlife Area is situated adjacent to private lands and a local dahlia farm and highlights the importance of integrating habitat restoration with riparian conservation. By addressing the needs of both wildlife and the surrounding community, the unit serves as a model for sustainable natural resource management, contributing to the long-term health of the Bogachiel River ecosystem and its diverse ecosystems.

Stone from the River: Wynoochee
by Carolyn Maddux

blue-gray sandstone
roughly oval
smoothed by the river
to a matte finish
from a gravel bar
in the river
from a pool
below the dam
from the leavings
of a glacier
from the ocean floor
thrust upward
traveling through time
sharing space
with the hooves of elk and deer
feet of bear and otter
thrust of kingfisher and heron
spawn of salmon
shifting downstream
toward warmer water
less water
smoke and wildfire
fewer fish
sudden floods
back toward
the ocean floor

Bogachiel: Anderson Homestead
by Carolyn Maddux

Like other rivers flowing west from the Olympic Mountains
— Quinault, Queets, and Hoh — the Bogachiel has carved
and scoured a valley broad and green, fed for years the fields
of this old ranchland sanctuary. Heavy rains and snow-melt
fill the river brimful, carving, carrying silt that settles at the edges.
Deer and elk graze water-meadows lush with forbs and grasses.
In the spring, the land is loud with tree-frog choruses, warblers,
and the tangled song of dippers as they bob and forage in
the rushing water.

Each fall's rains swell rivers just in time
for salmon runs. The spawners make their way upstream
to reproduce and die; their carcasses feed bears and eagles,
water creatures, and the hatchling fish.
In springtime, deep pools in the cool
of forest shade shelter swirling trout and steelhead;
salmonid fingerlings feed and grow and hide
from hungry herons and kingfishers, ready to make their way
downstream. In summer, as the season warms,
streams flowing from lofty Bogachiel Peak,
the High Divide and Seven Lakes Basin rise, each
afternoon, milky-green with minerals as mountain
snowfields melt.

And each year glaciers melt
and shrink, and snowfields disappear.
Aquifers decline, and streams diminish.
More fires burn the forest every year.
Shallow water warms until the
warmth becomes a barrier
and young fish float belly-up. Without the
salmon runs, the forest is less fertile.
Native grasses will fail to grow. Invasive
species will move in, and grazing animals
struggle to find fodder. Predators,

bear and cougar, fisher and weasel,
eagle and hawk, will thrive for a time
on weakened prey, but soon
their numbers, too,
will dwindle.

And then when
winters come
with no snow
on the mountains,
we might see
these big rivers
shrivel down
to become
just
seasonal
streams.

Elk May Safely Graze: The Wishkah
        after J.S. Bach
by Carolyn Maddux

Safe in the game fields the elk are grazing,
Munching at night, in the morning lazing
Here, where the grass is planted
So they won't graze unwanted,
Won't fashion a trampled playfield
Out of some farmer's hayfield.

        Foraging free, in safe Wishkah meadows,
        Bulls and cows content, and predators rare,
        Calves growing fast on the places' green fare—
        Just if it gets no drier,
        Just if there's no wildfire—
        Thriving on the game department's care.

Salmon swim upstream at end of summers,
Down to the sea go the hatchling swimmers,
Rains fill the running river
But there is no forever:
Seasons are rearranging
Now that the climate's changing.

        Summers grow warmer, season by season,
        Winter snows are less and wetter, year after year.
        Fire seasons sometimes start in springtime here.
        Once mossy rainforests
        Rang with a froggy chorus
        Now the summers leave them parched and sere.

Futures don't bother the Wishkah elk herds,
Deer and the bears and the busy songbirds.
Ruminants don't consider
Whether the snows deliver,
Whether the streams keep running.
(We - we should have seen it coming.)

Elk, with the Wishkah flowing by swiftly,
Feed at peace today, away from all woe,
Tall orchard grass and succulent clover grow
Well cultivated for them
Entrances gated for them
Safe enough till hunting season starts,
Safe enough till hunting season starts.

PUGET LOWLAND ECOREGION

Puget Lowland Ecoregion
Poet Rena Priest

Skagit Wildlife Area
Poet Jessica Gigot

Scatter Creek Wildlife Area
Poet Ann Batchelor Hursey

Puget Lowland Ecoregion

The Puget Lowland Ecoregion encompasses the lands along Puget Sound in Washington, extending across eastern Vancouver Island and the areas adjacent to the Strait of Georgia in British Columbia. The region's mild maritime climate, characterized by warm, dry summers and mild, wet winters, sustains a diversity of plant and animal life. Spanning forested lowlands, estuaries, freshwater systems, and prairies, the landscape is bordered by the Cascade Range to the east and the Olympic Mountains to the west, creating a dynamic environment shaped by both topographic and climatic factors.

Historically dominated by dense coniferous forests of Douglas-fir and western hemlock, the ecoregion also includes riparian habitat, wetlands, South Puget Sound prairies, and estuarine environments. These diverse habitats provide essential habitat for a wide array of terrestrial, aquatic, and marine species, including salmon spawning grounds, nesting sites for migratory birds, and marine habitat for mammals like orcas and seals. However, urban development and suburban sprawl, especially in the populous areas around Seattle and Tacoma, have significantly altered these landscapes, increasing pressure on ecosystems.

The Puget Lowland Ecoregion is increasingly affected by climate change, with sea-level rise impacting nearshore ecosystems critical for salmon, shorebirds, and forage fish. Many of these habitats have already been fragmented by human modifications to the nearshore, including diking, shoreline armoring, and development. These changes limit the ability of coastal habitats to migrate landward in response to rising seas, increasing the risk of habitat loss. The loss of intertidal wetlands and other nearshore habitats reduces the ability of these systems to buffer against coastal flooding, exacerbating risks to both ecological and human communities.

The Puget Lowland Ecoregion's hydrology is undergoing significant changes due to a warming climate, with cascading effects on freshwater availability, flood risks, and ecosystem resilience. As temperatures continue to rise, a greater proportion of winter precipitation will fall as rain rather than snow, particularly in mid-elevation basins that historically accumulated seasonal snowpack. This shift will contribute to a decline in overall snowpack, which has traditionally played a crucial role in regulating water availability throughout the year.

This transformation of the region's hydrology is expected to result in higher winter streamflows and increased flood risks, as more precipitation falls as rain, leading to more runoff. At the same time, spring snowmelt will occur earlier in the year, reducing the availability of water during the summer months when demand is highest. These shifts will lead to drier summer conditions and increased moisture stress across the region, affecting both aquatic and terrestrial ecosystems.

These hydrological changes will have widespread impacts, particularly for cold-water-dependent species such as salmon and steelhead, which rely on stable streamflows and cool water temperatures. As summer flows decline and stream temperatures rise, these species will face greater challenges in their migration, spawning, and survival. Additionally, terrestrial ecosystems will experience increased drought stress, altering vegetation patterns and habitat availability for wildlife.

Understanding and preparing for these shifts will be critical in ensuring the long-term resilience of both human and ecological communities in the Puget Sound region. While the Puget Lowland remains one of the most developed ecoregions in Washington, restoration efforts and nature-based solutions will be essential for increasing ecosystem resilience in the face of climate change. By focusing on habitat connectivity, climate-informed restoration, and protecting and enhancing natural floodplains, wetlands, and riparian systems, this region can maintain ecological function, support biodiversity, and build resilience to a changing climate.

Whatcom Creek—A Lummi Fishing Village
Kwot = Waters; Kwem = Strong or loud
by Rena Priest

Now, what can be said? And who should explain?
About the noisy torrent, full of life—
It's not that it's gone. But it's not the same.
I never saw it in full strength, so grief
finds me on its banks, washes me away
to longing for these waters to reclaim
their voice, their roaring, their natural way.
That power from which this place takes its name
is now but a mumble, dredged to make way
for who cares what? And the salmon that run
are hatchery-raised, so people can say
"Look! Look at all the worthy things we've done."
Yes, it's true; a salmon run still returns
to this place, where a ghost village still burns.

Skagit Wildlife Area

The Skagit Wildlife Area encompasses over 18,000 acres of diverse wildlife habitat across Skagit, Island, Snohomish, and San Juan counties. This area includes intertidal estuaries, managed agricultural lands, and native habitats, with many units located near Skagit, Padilla, and Port Susan bays or along the Skagit River. These habitats provide critical forage and cover for wintering waterfowl, as well as habitat for bald eagles, salmon, owls, and various other species. The mixing of fresh and saltwater in this region creates a unique estuary ecosystem, which is managed and restored to support both wildlife and human access.

One of the key units within the Skagit Wildlife Area is the Leque Island Unit, located between Port Susan and Skagit Bays. With a mix of intertidal and estuarine habitats, the unit supports a wide range of species, including ducks, swans, songbirds, salmon, and harbor seals. Recreation opportunities are numerous, with visitors enjoying activities such as wildlife viewing, photography, hiking along the Eide Road trail, and waterfowl hunting. The Davis Slough Boat Launch, located on the unit's western boundary, provides access to the Skagit Bay Estuary and Puget Sound.

Caption for photo previous spread: Gray whales feeding on ghost shrimp in Port Susan, Washington. During high tide, these whales move close to shore, roll onto their sides, and suck up mouthfuls of sediment, filtering out tiny invertebrates for food. Photo credit: Harriet Morgan.

Leque Island has undergone a transformative restoration effort to revive its natural estuary ecosystem and enhance climate resilience. Historically a salt marsh, the island was converted to farmland through diking in the late 1800s. In 1974, WDFW began acquiring parcels of the island, eventually integrating it into the Skagit Wildlife Area. Recognizing the importance of the site for both ecological and community resilience, WDFW collaborated with Ducks Unlimited, the Stillaguamish Tribe, The Nature Conservancy, and the Skagit River System Cooperative to restore tidal marsh habitat in the Stillaguamish River estuary.

The project, completed in phases from 2019 to 2022, removed 3 miles of dikes, excavated over 5 miles of new tidal channels, and reconnected nearly 276 acres of tidal marsh to natural estuarine flows. These restored wetlands now serve as critical habitat for juvenile Chinook salmon, which depend on estuaries during their transition from freshwater to marine environments. By supporting Chinook salmon populations, the project also contributes to the recovery of Southern Resident killer whales, which rely on these fish for survival. Additionally, the revitalized marshes now sustain a diverse array of wildlife, including shorebirds and waterfowl.

Beyond ecological restoration, the project enhances the region's resilience to climate change. Tidal marshes act as natural buffers against coastal and river flooding by absorbing and slowing runoff, stabilizing riverbanks, dissipating wave energy, and serving as physical barriers. At Leque Island, the restored tidal marshes help reduce the severity of flood damage, protecting both ecological assets and vulnerable infrastructure. These benefits align with broader goals of mitigating climate impacts, such as increased flooding intensity and sea-level rise, while offering recreational amenities like walking trails, parking, and a hand boat launch. This innovative project exemplifies how habitat restoration can simultaneously address climate challenges, bolster biodiversity, and strengthen community ties to Washington's unique ecosystems.

Aerial comparison of the Leque Island Restoration Project site before and after dike removal. The top image (2017) shows the site before restoration, with dikes restricting tidal flow and heavily channelizing the landscape. The bottom image (2022), taken three years after the dike breach, highlights restored tidal channels and natural processes. While the images are taken from different angles, the agricultural field in the right serves as a spatial reference point. This project reconnects hundreds of acres of tidal marsh, improving habitat for salmon, shorebirds, and other wildlife while enhancing climate resilience. Photo credits: WDFW.

Restoration Pantoum
by Jessica Gigot
          —*Leque Island*, 2024

At low tide, in spring, we walk to the island's wild edge.
Follow the berm that protects the town from waves.
The root of restore is to give back, renew.
Three men diked the island, farmed the fertile soil.

The new berm supports waves of dog walkers, passing hunters.
Old snags sink down in estuarine mud—we scramble.
Once diked and farmed, this fertile island now begins a feral story.
Five miles of new channels support habitat for fish and birds.

We scramble over old snags, boots sink in estuary-gray mud.
A seal head, slick and dark, pops up in the river then dives down.
Juvenile salmon, like Chinook, habitually rely on these channels.
Can these changes beget more and better change?

I see a colony of scrubby heron nests across the river.
At high tide, in fall, the island fills like a bay—
a song of returning that might someday sing itself.
Restore means we must go back, to make anew.

Scatter Creek Wildlife Area

The Scatter Creek Wildlife Area, located in southwestern Washington, spans diverse ecosystems including prairies, oak woodlands, conifer forests, and riparian areas along Scatter Creek. Managed by WDFW, the area plays a critical role in managing rare habitats and supporting a variety of wildlife species. Once common in the South Puget Sound region, prairies and oak woodlands have declined dramatically, with just 3% of prairie extent remaining. These ecosystems, formed 15,000 years ago by retreating glaciers, are among the rarest in the country. Conservation efforts at Scatter Creek focus on protecting fragile prairie habitat and supporting species such as the Mazama pocket gopher, Oregon spotted frog, and Taylor's checkerspot butterfly. The wildlife area also provides opportunities for recreational activities like hiking, wildlife viewing, and hunting, while navigating the complex challenge of balancing diverse public uses with the critical need for conservation and multi-species recovery in a rapidly urbanizing region.

The Scatter Creek Wildlife Area is a critical component of the wildlife area, as it contains the unique South Puget Sound prairie ecosystem, with prairie grasses and wildflowers that support pollinators and other wildlife. Restoration efforts focus on reducing invasive species, managing fire regimes, and enhancing habitat for sensitive species. In addition to its ecological importance, the unit offers educational and recreational opportunities for visitors to experience one of Washington's rarest and most threatened ecosystems.

Indigenous burning practices, or cultural burns, have long been an integral part of managing the prairies and oak woodlands of the South Puget Sound region, including the Scatter Creek Wildlife Area. Indigenous peoples of the Pacific Northwest used low-intensity burns to maintain open prairie ecosystems, enhance soil health, and facilitate the growth of edible and culturally significant plants, such as camas. While the primary purpose of these burns was to sustain these habitats and support culturally important species, they also had the added benefit of controlling woody vegetation and invasive species while enhancing habitat for key species. This traditional ecological knowledge is increasingly being recognized and adopted by western science based approaches for sustainable land management.

Building on these practices, WDFW has reintroduced prescribed fire as a cornerstone of habitat restoration on Scatter Creek's prairies. Prescribed burns not only reduce invasive plants and restore native grasses and flowers but also improve conditions for wildlife species that depend on these rare ecosystems. For instance, recent burns at Scatter Creek have helped promote the recovery of Taylor's checkerspot butterfly by regenerating the native vegetation that provides nectar-rich flowers for butterflies and host plants essential for caterpillars.

While Western science has only recently begun to recognize the role of fire in maintaining prairie ecosystems, Indigenous communities have long used cultural burning to sustain biodiversity and ecosystem health. Acknowledging this knowledge, WDFW is working to integrate fire as a management tool in prairie restoration, supporting resilient landscapes for future generations.

Building on restoration efforts like prescribed burns, researchers at WDFW and the University of Washington are investigating how habitat diversity at the Scatter Creek Wildlife Area can support climate resilience for at-risk butterfly species in the Pacific Northwest.

Despite extensive recovery efforts for species like Taylor's checkerspot, Oregon silverspot, Fender's blue, and mardon skipper, questions remain about how to design habitats that help them adapt to climate change. One key factor is habitat diversity, which includes variations in vegetation types, microclimates, and structural features such as sunny and shaded areas, moist and dry patches, and different plant heights. These elements create a mosaic of conditions that butterflies can use to meet their needs as environmental conditions shift.

(above) Biologists survey for mardon skipper butterflies at Scatter Creek Wildlife Area. Photo credit: WDFW.

(left) WDFW staff blacklining—pre-burning a controlled strip to establish a firebreak and prevent unintended fire spread—at the Scatter Creek Wildlife Area in July 2024. Blacklining is a key step in prescribed fire operations, which WDFW has reintroduced as a habitat restoration tool to reduce invasive plants, promote native vegetation, and improve conditions for species like Taylor's checkerspot butterfly. Photo credit: WDFW.

For example, during extreme heat, butterflies may seek shade or cooler microclimates, while in cooler periods, sunlit areas provide warmth. Nectar plants blooming at different times ensure food availability throughout the season, and a mix of host plants supports successful reproduction. By assessing restoration efforts at Scatter Creek, researchers aim to determine whether current habitat conditions are effectively providing these diverse features and how they influence butterfly survival.

Findings from this work will inform science-based habitat management strategies to enhance climate resilience for butterflies and other sensitive species. As rising temperatures and extreme weather reshape ecosystems, this research will help guide conservation practices to ensure these species remain part of Washington's natural heritage.

An adult Taylor's checkerspot butterfly rests on a flower. Photo credit: WDFW.

Nativity Must be Present for Balsamroot to Grow.*
by Ann Batchelor Hursey

Nativity, as in what habitat was like before European settlers
homesteaded this oak prairie on Chehalis ancestral lands.

Restoration took twenty years to revive this nativity.
Workers cut down fast growing firs, and with prescribed

burns, removed invasive woody plants like scotch broom,
replacing it with native grasses like Roemer's fescue.

Today Chehalis women harvest camas and balsamroot.
Balsamroot, with its bright yellow faces and thick

arrow-shaped leaves grows in foot tall clumps. Rumors
say these small sunflowers smell like chocolate.

I bend my head to inhale yellow petals and smell only
damp earth and grass. As I slowly stand to get my balance,

two small butterflies, blue as the camas flower, fly past.
This prairie births thousands of camas and Blue-eyed Marys

whose blue and purple petals reclaim the land. Yellow buttercups
dot the prairie. Last night's puddles reflect the blue above.

I return to the trail and see one garter snake sunning itself.
My presence startles the silence. He wriggles away

hidden by grass, back to the creek
where salmon eggs rest, ready to hatch.

Unless, like last summer's drought—

Scatter Creek dried-up.
1500 coho smolt died-out.

---

* *a quote from Bill Kronland, WA Fish and Wildlife biologist*

Tribal Restoration of Scatter Creek Prairie
by Ann Batchelor Hursey

Tribal members invited me to join them as they gathered ironwood
for next year's root-digging sticks. In late June, we walked through

knee-high dry grass to the prairie's edge. William found us dry
camas seed pods. We cupped their tiny cargo of seeds in our hands.

These seeds, future camas bulbs. We spread out to harvest
ironwood, also known as ocean spray. William reminded us how

ironwood often grows near camas. Its elegant and sturdy boughs
resist sharp pruning saws. To cut a bough requires strength and focus.

Our group of seven harvested two dozen. With help from Dan,
I harvested one. These fresh-cut digging sticks need time to cure.

Next April, a tribal elder will teach a class on how to shape
and create new root-digging sticks for May's camas harvest.

The Chehalis have harvested these roots since time immemorial.
Just three percent of their prairie's left for harvesting camas.

Even as the earth's temperature rises, the Chehalis find ways to
steward these prairies they call home. They know summer's

ironwood gathering teaches future generations about digging sticks,
a traditional tool for next year's camas harvest.

Each harvest, a lesson.
Each seed, a promise.

You Cannot Talk about Scatter Creek Prairie
without Talking about the Chehalis River
by Ann Batchelor Hursey

        I.   Chehalis Means "My Wealth is Water"

Scatter Creek flows into the Chehalis Basin and merges into
the Chehalis River, Washington State's last wild and free river.

The Chehalis know that all land adjacent to the river, its prairies
and forests marbled with creeks, contribute to its health.

This glacial outwash prairie occupies a part of Chehalis homelands,
whose rain-fed rivers flow west from the mountains into the sea.

The Chehalis have stewarded these fire-adapted prairies, called them
"our grocery store," harvested roots and berries, lured elk, and deer to
graze.

They understand how seasons bring both floods and the salmon's return.
Grateful for both spring and autumn salmon runs.

Four salmon species call this flood plain home for spawning:
coho, chum, steelhead, chinook. The warming air brings heavy rains,

more flooding. How do we sustain this last wild and free river?
Chehalis, the name of its People and its river that brings wealth.

        II. One-hundred Year Floods Happen Every Four

The temperature is rising. Rain is more frequent and flooding, a fact.
Mudslides from clear cuts clog the rivers, blocking the salmon.

Some believe that oaks hold conversations with their prairie relations like
balsamroot and camas, reassure them that their slow-growing roots

and limbs will help to hold water in the sandy soil, help shade
the chrysalis of butterflies, the burrows of Mazama pocket gophers,

allow blossoms of Blue-eyed Marys to assist pollinators.
We know that prairie restoration helps to amplify this dialog

among all living things. Oaks thrive when prescribed burns
keep the prairies open from invasive plants like Douglas fir.

Species have a chance to navigate toward cooler prairies north.
The rain will keep falling. The Chehalis say let the land be resilient:

remove dams on the Skookumchuck and the Wynoochee Rivers.
Let the glacial contours from the past do their work.

Let the rain flow free down salmon-spawning rivers.
Let the Chehalis harvest camas root and balsamroot.

Let prairies hold green conversations with the future.

N.B. *Some research drawn from* Chehalis: A Watershed Moment, *Documentary,*
Cascade PBS, 2020 Not Rated 1 hr 2 m
With gratitude to:
Bill Kronland, Scatter Creek Wildlife Manager, Region 6
William Thoms, Cultural Resource Specialist, Chehalis Tribe
Dan Penn, Tribal Historic Preservation Officer

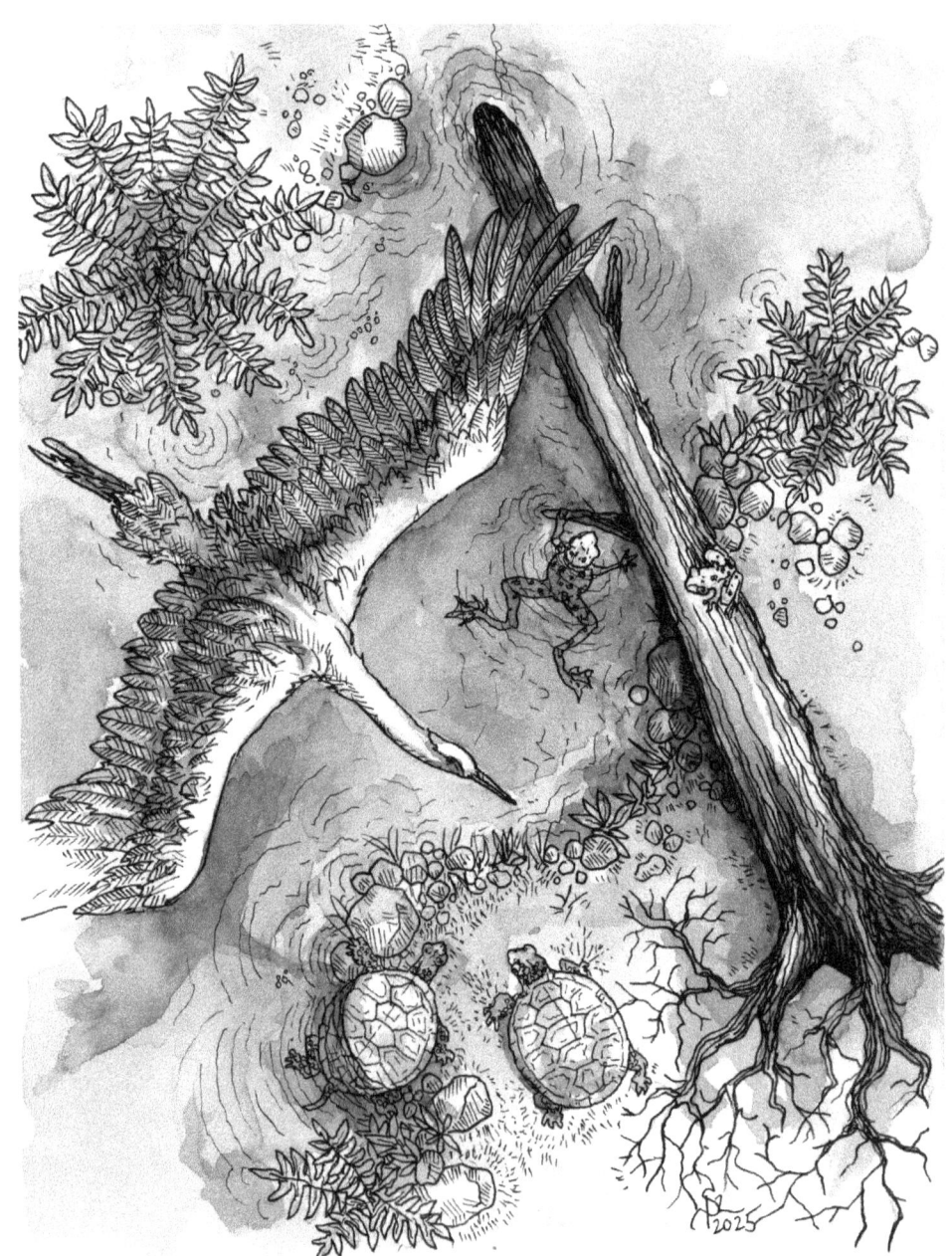

WILLAMETTE VALLEY ECOREGION

Willamette Valley Ecoregion
Poet Julian Ankney

Mount Saint Helens Wildlife Area
Poets Kathleen Byrd and Simmons Buntin

Shillapoo Wildlife Area
Poet Scot Siegel

Willamette Valley Ecoregion

Nestled between the Coast Range and the Cascades, the Willamette Valley is a broad plain of rolling hills, fertile soils, and diverse habitats. At its northern boundary in Washington, the region is shaped by the convergence of the Lewis and Columbia Rivers, while most of the Willamette Valley ecoregion lies within northwestern Oregon. Its Mediterranean-like climate, with warm, dry summers and mild, wet winters, historically supported prairies, oak savannas, wetlands, and forests. However, ecological changes such as altered fire regimes, floodplain dynamics, and invasive species have significantly impacted habitats in the region.

The Columbia and Willamette Rivers have played a key role in shaping the valley's hydrology, with extensive braided river channels and floodplains that absorbed high water flows, replenished wetlands, maintained consistent stream flows, and regulated water temperatures. However, channelization, diking, and wetland drainage have significantly reduced floodplain connectivity, limiting these rivers' ability to mitigate flooding and retain water during the drier summer months. Restoring these connections is crucial for climate resilience, as healthy floodplains store excess water, reduce downstream flood risks, and provide refuge for fish and wildlife in an increasingly variable climate.

Invasive species further compound these challenges by outcompeting native vegetation and reducing habitat quality. Scotch broom, Himalayan blackberry, and reed canarygrass thrive in disturbed or degraded areas, preventing the regeneration of native prairies and wetlands. These species are often aided by warming temperatures and altered precipitation patterns, making them increasingly difficult to control. Their spread reduces food and shelter for native wildlife, including pollinators and grassland-dependent birds, while also increasing fire risk in some areas.

Efforts to restore the Willamette Valley's ecosystems—including removing invasive species and re-establishing floodplain connectivity—are essential to building resilience in the face of climate change. By improving habitat quality and restoring natural hydrologic processes, these actions support biodiversity, protect water resources, and enhance the valley's ability to adapt to shifting environmental conditions.

Net Zero
by Julian Ankney

At the end of the oregon trail, 'Nchi Wana's mouth
 the vulnerable Golden Paintbrush and alluvial soil
  live, a prairie and a valley, the Willamette

a Nez Perce word meaning
 the rim of a Basket, a binding
  a hem, the brim of a hat

an edge, a border, they say
 They say in that valley, the Willamette
   Coyote made his Magic Fish Trap

he built Willamette Falls there
 where the Willamette Daisy, now endangered
  Upriver Chinook Salmon now too

Lower Columbia River Salmon, "*wéetu*"
 no Coho, no Snake River Chinook
  "*wéetu*" Sockeye or Steelhead, a Tipping Point

When Coyote's trap would became full of fish
 it would say "*Noseepsk!*" They say in Clackmas Chinook
  indeed the trap was full of salmon long long ago

When the earth was yet becoming from, Fire and Flame,
Molten In the Belly Of Monsters
  They lived there

"Noseepsk! Noseepsk!" the Fish Trap would say to Coyote
 Coyote annoyed at all the fish piling in it and having to get them
   became angry with the trap and said

"Can't you wait with your fish catching until I've built this fire?"
 thenceforth the Magic Fish Trap refused to catch fish
  from that day on

The People had to spear their prized fish, they say
 Now measured by carbon footprints
  and not the removal of Northern Red-legged Frog

"wéetu'" No- not the Foothill Yellow-legged Frog
 Nor the Northwestern Pond Turtle
  Western Meadowlark or Western Bluebird, almost gone

warmer waters and fossil fuels mitigate biodiversity
 Boulders Erratics and Tomanowos and Spirits to be
  Nature-based solutions are intergenerational

rights, they say, are build from Land but come from Water
as Grey Wolf and Shaggy Horkelia will tell you
if you listen, they say

"*Noseepsk!*"
the fish came back, only after the People were gone
  "*Noseepsk!*" they say

(above) The South Bachelor Island Restoration Project in Clark County, Washington, relocated approximately 120,000 cubic yards of sand dredged from the Columbia River to restore off-channel habitat for salmon. This shallow-water area provides critical stopover locations for migrating juvenile salmon, allowing them to rest and improving their chances of survival as they journey to the ocean. Photo credit: WDFW.

(next spread) The Two Forks Unit of the Mount St. Helens Wildlife Area, located at the confluence of the North and East forks of the Lewis River, provides essential freshwater and riparian habitat for songbirds, fish, and other wildlife. Its mature black cottonwood forest supports biodiversity, while the river serves as a key migratory pathway and rearing habitat for salmon. Photo credit: Harriet Morgan.

Mount Saint Helens Wildlife Area

The Mount St. Helens Wildlife Area spans over 10,000 acres across Clark, Cowlitz, Skamania, and Wahkiakum counties in southwest Washington. With units ranging from 20 to 3,816 acres and elevations varying from sea-level to 1,800 feet, the area supports a diverse range of habitats, including tidal mudflats, wetlands, riparian zones, old-growth and early seral mixed forests, ancient lava flows, and open grasslands. The largest units—Hoffstadt, Mudflow, and Merrill Lake—provide critical winter range habitat for a portion of the Mount St. Helens elk herd and support threatened and endangered salmon species. Most units are open to the public, offering opportunities for wildlife viewing, hunting, and fishing, with seasonal access restrictions in place to protect sensitive species. The Two Forks Unit, a 49-acre area at the confluence of the North and East forks of the Lewis River, is managed primarily for songbirds within its mature black cottonwood riparian forest, while also providing habitat for Columbian white-tailed deer and essential migratory pathways for anadromous salmonids.

The Eagle Island Unit, part of the Mount Saint Helens Wildlife Area, spans 279 acres along the North Fork Lewis River in Clark and Cowlitz counties, about 5 miles east of Woodland. Acquired in 2011 through a grant from Washington's Recreation and Conservation Office, this unit is accessible only by boat and features a mix of floodplain, riparian forest, and open meadow habitats. It is managed to support a range of wildlife and aquatic species, including salmonids, black-tailed deer, waterfowl, songbirds, and birds of prey. The island serves as critical habitat for fish migration, juvenile rearing, and spawning, as well as a potential enhancement site for band-tailed pigeons.

Wildlife area staff recently focused conservation efforts on Eagle Island, a 230-acre unit of the Mount Saint Helens Wildlife Area, by removal of invasive Scotch broom and by enhancing its grassland habitat with native pollinator seeds. The project involved spreading a mix of wildflower and native grass seeds across bare areas on the island, thanks to a generous native seed donation from the Cowlitz Noxious Weed Control Board and Washington State Noxious Weed Control Board. While the wildflowers are expected to take up to two years to bloom and set seed, the goal is for these native plants to establish themselves, fill in the grasslands, and naturally spread to adjacent areas over time. Their work supports the restoration of native ecosystems on Eagle Island, which is already teeming with wildlife such as eagles, ducks, and deer.

Pollinator habitats in Washington are increasingly under threat from habitat loss, widespread use of pesticides and herbicides, and the impacts of climate change. Rising temperatures and drier summer conditions associated with climate change are exacerbating these challenges, making it more difficult for native pollinators to thrive. Additionally, climate change is expected to facilitate the spread and establishment of invasive species, such as Scotch broom, which is already prevalent in Western Washington. Scotch broom is expected to be directly favored under changing precipitation and temperature patterns, allowing it to outcompete native plants and degrade the quality of pollinator habitats. This underscores the urgency of pollinator habitat restoration, which is essential for boosting climate resilience. Restored habitats provide native plants that support larger, more stable pollinator populations, enabling them to better adapt to environmental changes while maintaining their critical role in ecosystems and agriculture.

Pollinator habitat restoration, such as the grassland restoration efforts at Eagle Island using native pollinator seeds, plays a vital role in enhancing climate resilience and promoting overall ecosystem health. By removing invasive species and reintroducing native plants to grassland habitats, these efforts not only provide essential resources for pollinators but also help create more adaptive and stable ecosystems capable of withstanding the impacts of climate change.

Questions for a River
by Simmons Buntin

> —*Confluence of the North and East Forks of the Lewis River,*
> *Two Forks Wildlife Area, Washington*

1. Where are your headwaters?

   On the western slope of a fiery throat.

2. Where do you end?

   There is no end, there is only flow.

3. How do you flow?

   Upriver, dammed—
   but here, at last, the full body of myself.

4. Who swims in your waters?

   Salmon and salmon peoples.

5. Who else swims in your waters?

   Lamprey and longfin, mussel and midge,
   mother and daughter, father and son.

6. Where is your voice?

   Beneath propellor and keel, my chorus is strong—
   the powerboats have not always muffled my song.

7. Who sings from your shore?

   Have you heard the belted kingfisher's morning trill?
   The song sparrow's lyric in the evening still?
   The *treep* and *click* of the dipper seeking her fill?

8. How do you rage?

In the storm's sweet fury, or
patiently, for all bridges and levees eventually fail.

9. What have you learned?

Flow is the highest form of being.

10. And what have you learned?

We all are part of the savaged sea.

Across the River
by Simmons Buntin

—Lewis River, Two Forks Wildlife Area, Washington

If there's anything
to lift you
from your knees,
damp from plumbing
the modest white
petals of common marsh
bedstraw & further
down the pure &
pungent loam itself,
it's the cry
of a bald eagle
across the river,
shadow among evergreens
risen above park &
pasture, above
the river & its ribbon
of cottonwoods & poplar,
above even the awful
whine of Sea-
Doos weaving
from bank to bank.
What wouldn't you give
to mute those motors,
the rowers & rafters,
the waders & wailers?
How long will you
long for one more cry
between the river &
its cacophonous sky?

Safe Passage
by Kathleen Byrd

—A poem for the Two Forks Wildlife Area Unit of the Mount Saint Helen's
Wildlife Areas (primarily managed for songbirds)

Every interstate overpass has an understory.
This particular one is part of the I-5 corridor
that passes North to South from Canada through California
                                        following the coast line.

Under the overpass, a confluence, and noise. Noise that drowns the
   sounds of songbirds
that drowns the sounds of two rivers meeting on their passage to the Sea.

Rivers have purposes that are only part mystery to us.

                    Rivers need
                                to meander & wend
                                        to obey gravity.
                        Rivers need
                                obstacles.
(there are so few words for water)

I surveyed the scene: Concrete, graffiti, trash, the rumble of a logging
   truck passing overhead,
an old Mustang at the entrance to the wildlife area.
Leaning against the Mustang, a bicycle. Someone's home.

In this dissonant eddy, I sat in my car and wondered.
How does a poet find words to make something sacred of the desecrated?

But the sacred is always right there. Right here,
an undercurrent.

The rivers are poems
   carrying ancient stories
      of Loowit and Klickitat - sacred guides - the distant mountains,
        moving mulch and mineral,
          Elk and Bear
            in scat and saliva
              carrying them all downstream
                to mingle in the ongoingness
                  of water.

What do we know of the sentience of rivers? Of the sacrifices they make?
The language of rivers is not words
          but water
             is time
(no hurtling toward a future).
      A river is murmur and roar
         is ripple and tumble
           making sound out of stone.
     These rivers have sacred names: Cathlapotle and Yahkotl.

(I think you can hear water in your mouth when you say them)
Nothing is ever lost though you may not hear it (because of the noise).

I too traveled the interstate in a vehicle of steel on my way here.
The Salmon journey up river
       swimming against the current.
             Their whole lives a sacrifice,
        a pilgrimage, a journey
          of muscle and blood
            fat and bone.

The language of salmon is breath in the gills, thrash in the current.
You might not hear it (because of the noise).
What we know of this is only what we know.
And what we know is never
not ever
settled.

The land here was "settled", homesteaded, and renamed
 but the wild stays in the understory.
The past is not lost in the present. The rivers remember their original names.
There are People who remember.

The oaks in the lowlands have a language that is not words
but a geometry of roots that grow deep and wide under earth
and skyward in branches that cast shadows,
shadows that protect the salmon as they journey upriver.

In the end, the oaks bend their long arms back to earth, nourishing
  what's next.
Perhaps the song birds translate their language into sound (for us).
We can hear it (despite the noise).

Under the noise of the interstate is nourishment
is protection of rivers, riparian habitat,
old Oregon Oaks, and Black Cottonwood forests
promising safe passage for salmon and songbirds.

It is not quiet here
there are no white-tailed deer
(who intelligently avoid the noise)
                         but the river continues
                                    and the salmon journey
                                         and some people protect
and a poet's words are a prayer
a prayer for safe passage for all beings
for all our wild-life journeys.

Shillapoo Wildlife Area

The Shillapoo Wildlife Area, located in the Columbia River floodplain in Clark County, provides critical breeding, wintering, and migratory habitats for a wide array of wildlife. Spanning approximately 2,420 acres, Shillapoo supports species like Canada geese, mallards, and other dabbling ducks, as well as mink, great blue heron, black-capped chickadee, western meadowlark, and yellow warbler. Additionally, the area's aquatic habitats are vital for threatened and endangered salmonid species, including Lower Columbia coho, Chinook salmon, Columbia River chum salmon, Snake River sockeye, and steelhead, which depend on nearby waterways like the Columbia River, Lake River, and Vancouver Lake for spawning and rearing.

Two chum salmon navigate shallow water during their upstream migration to freshwater spawning grounds, where they will lay eggs in gravel nests called redds. After spawning, the salmon will complete their lifecycle, dying in the stream and decomposing—returning essential nutrients to the ecosystem and supporting the next generation of fish, wildlife, and aquatic plants. Photo credit: Harriet Morgan.

Shillapoo is part of the Pacific Flyway, one of the major migratory bird routes in North America. Stretching from Alaska to South America, the Pacific Flyway links breeding, stopover, and wintering habitats that are essential for millions of migratory birds each year. This vast corridor supports over 400 bird species, including waterfowl, shorebirds, raptors, and songbirds, all of which rely on high-quality habitats like Shillapoo for food, rest, and shelter during their journeys. Within the flyway, Shillapoo serves as a key wintering site, supporting over 200,000 waterfowl during the winter and more than 300,000 during migration periods. The area also functions as a staging ground for the state-endangered sandhill crane during spring and fall migrations, with some cranes overwintering in the area. Bald eagles, federally listed as threatened, nest in adjacent lands and are present in large numbers during winter. The Shillapoo North and South units are popular spots for waterfowl hunting and offer excellent viewing opportunities for species like sandhill cranes, great blue herons, and a variety of waterfowl.

(above) Sandhill cranes forage in the open fields of Shillapoo Wildlife Area. Located along the Pacific Flyway, this site provides critical stopover habitat for migratory birds, offering food and rest during their long seasonal journeys. Photo credit: Harriet Morgan.

(next page) WDFW, with assistance from the Washington Department of Natural Resources, conducted prescribed burns in fall 2021 at the North and South units of the Shillapoo Wildlife Area in Clark County. These controlled burns targeted invasive vegetation such as reed canary grass and Himalayan blackberry to improve habitat quality and support native plant restoration. Photo credit: WDFW.

Climate change has the potential to affect the timing of migration along the Pacific Flyway, which may impact species' access to critical resources at key stopover sites like Shillapoo. Changes in temperatures and seasonal patterns could alter the availability of food and habitat, highlighting the value of preserving and restoring areas like Shillapoo to support healthy populations. These habitats play a crucial role in migration by providing reliable resting and refueling stops for birds during their long journeys, especially for species that synchronize their movements with food availability across vast distances.

Management at Shillapoo reflects a balance between agricultural practices and habitat restoration to sustain wildlife. Sharecropping and grazing agreements leave standing crops like corn and small grains as forage for waterfowl and sandhill cranes, while long-term plans aim to restore agricultural lands to wetland habitats. Prescribed burns are also used to manage invasive species like reed canary grass and Himalayan blackberry, improving habitat conditions for waterfowl and other wildlife. These burns help maintain open wetland areas, reduce reliance on herbicides, and promote the growth of native vegetation. These efforts enhance Shillapoo's capacity to support migratory species, addressing challenges like invasive species, altered hydrology, and habitat loss. Through these efforts, the Shillapoo Wildlife Area plays an important role in supporting wildlife, addressing climate-related challenges, and preserving ecological balance.

Shillapoo Burn
by Scot Siegel

Forty-five degrees, humidity a pinprick
on your cheek when a breeze musses
the yellow cottonwood leaves, teasing
the steel wool sky. Perfect burning weather.

We wait as the burn boss checks for wind;
then she whistles the order to begin.
We tilt torch heads down. Blue tongues
touch brittle rafts of brown grass,

stoking a knee-wall of flame that wavers
and complains like a bag of bull snakes
after a light rain. Stumbling as it grows,
the fire noses furrows for pockets of oxygen,

sidestepping willows, folding in on itself
before slowly advancing, loving ragweed,
ravaging thistle, teasel, and reed canary grass;
invasives we're tasked with exterminating.

It will take decades for the restoration,
regeneration of native seedbeds in alluvium,
untethering of hydrology, re-creation of wetlands
and camas meadows, cold water refugia on the Columbia

for juvenile salmon and steelhead; a haven
on the flyway for sandhill cranes, snow geese,
grebes, and other migratory birds, who must feed
and rest as the west continues to heat up.

Now the wind shifts, and our crew pivots,
chasing errant embers that flirt with the oaks,
stomping them down before they can reach
the neighbor's farm. We work the head fire hard

nudging it towards a gravel bar, a break, a washboard
the grader made, a grave for flames,

final resting place for the controlled burn.

Shillapoo Haiku
by Scot Siegel

Winter cover crop
Buckwheat below the flyway –
Snow geese descending

~

Silage on the stalks
Free corn for migrating ducks
Plumping up for hunters

~

Across space and time
Sandhill cranes barbaric yawps
Pierce and pass through us

Mink
by Scot Siegel

Before fur farms or synthetics
Before dams and PCBs
Your wild fur commoditized
To near extinction.

But here you are in this backchannel.
Scrappy little carnivore
Are you foraging for frogs, or mice?
Whose home have you pillaged?

Did you take a skunk's hole for a den?
You might be royalty, my friend
Your non-monogamous ways,
Fecundity, and fifty-one days to gestation,

Growth potential, exponential!
Someday, your kind might retake this world.

NORTH CASCADES ECOREGION

Sinlahekin Wildlife Area
Poet Derek Sheffield

∽

Scotch Creek Wildlife Area
Poets Roger William Gilman
and Jill McCabe Johnson

North Cascades Ecoregion

The North Cascades Ecoregion spans the northern end of the Cascade Range, extending from northwest Washington into southern British Columbia, and includes the high Olympic Mountains to the west. This rugged landscape, defined by glaciated peaks, deep valleys, and headwater streams, supports some of Washington's most intact and biodiverse ecosystems. The region hosts the greatest concentration of active alpine glaciers in the contiguous United States, sustaining perennial streams and glacial lakes that are critical for wildlife and downstream communities. These ecosystems provide essential ecosystem services and serve as strongholds for biodiversity in the Pacific Northwest.

The ecoregion features pronounced differences between its western and eastern sides, shaped by climate and geography. On the west side, temperate maritime conditions bring annual precipitation ranging from 40 to over 100 inches, supporting cool forests dominated by western hemlock, Douglas fir, and western redcedar. Hardwood species such as red alder and bigleaf maple thrive in riparian areas. By contrast, the east side experiences a drier climate, with precipitation ranging from 50 inches near the crest to as little as 10 inches at lower elevations. This fosters open forests of ponderosa pine, grand fir, and western larch, with sagebrush and bluebunch wheatgrass occupying the lowest elevations. Higher elevations host subalpine forests of mountain hemlock and Pacific silver fir on the west and Engelmann spruce and subalpine larch on the east. These diverse habitats create a rich mosaic of ecosystems, supporting a wide array of species.

Climate change poses significant challenges for the North Cascades Ecoregion. Hotter, drier summers are expected to increase drought stress on plants and reduce water availability as soil moisture decreases earlier in the growing season. Snowpack plays a crucial role in replenishing water supplies during the spring and early summer and is projected to decrease, especially in mid-elevation areas near the winter freezing line. This loss of snowpack not only reduces water availability but also disrupts ecosystems, enabling trees to move into higher elevations while removing the insulating snow cover that cold-adapted species depend on for survival.

The role of wildfire in ecosystems differs significantly between Western and Eastern Washington. West of the Cascades, the maritime climate yields dense, productive, and long-lived wet forests that, historically, have experienced less frequent, mid- to high-severity wildfires (200 to 600 years between fires) that have burned thousands to hundreds –of thousands of acres. In specific areas, like the Olympic Peninsula's rain shadow and the Puget Lowland, fires occurred more frequently and with mixed severity, creating smaller patches of stand-replacing fire. In contrast, Eastern Washington's continental climate – drier, hotter summers and lower soil moisture—yields forests that are typically drier and less dense, with more space between trees. Eastern Washington has historically experienced frequent, low-severity fires that primarily burned the understory, cleaning out fuels but leaving fire-tolerant trees intact, allowing the forests to thrive despite these natural disturbances.

These fires were influenced by natural cycles and Indigenous fire stewardship practices, such as intentional burning. Indigenous burning helped maintain landscapes abundant in edible and culturally significant plants, such as blueberries, camas, and acorns. For thousands of years, Indigenous burning practices shaped fire-adapted ecosystems, maintaining forest health and enhancing biodiversity. However, colonization displaced Indigenous peoples and suppressed their cultural practices, including Indigenous burning. Over time, this suppression contributed to the development of formal fire exclusion and suppression policies—an approach that sought to eliminate fire from ecosystems rather than embrace its ecological role. Nearly a century of fire suppression has led to dense vegetation accumulation, significantly increasing the risk of large, high-severity fires in these forests. This problem is further compounded by warmer, drier summers driven by climate change, increasing the risk of large, severe wildfires, particularly in Eastern Washington.

Climate change has increased wildfire activity throughout the Western United States, a trend that is projected to accelerate with continued warming. Warmer, drier summers are expected to increase the risk of large wildfires across Washington. While Eastern Washington's forests are particularly vulnerable, even the wetter forests of Western Washington are at risk from increased area burned. Though wildfires are less common west of the Cascade crest, large and severe fires have occurred in the past and could happen again, with smaller, more frequent fires likely in the wildland-urban interface. These changes threaten ecosystems, local communities, and natural resources across the state.

A view of the North Cascades from Aasgard Pass in Washington's Alpine Lakes Wilderness, showcasing the ecoregion's complex topography and ecological gradients. Photo credit: Anour Esa.

Sinlahekin Wildlife Area

The Sinlahekin Wildlife Area, located in north-central Washington, is the oldest wildlife area managed by WDFW and was originally purchased for protecting mule deer winter range. Encompassing over 14,000 acres in the Okanogan Valley, the area is known for its striking shrubsteppe landscapes, mixed forests, and wetlands, which provide critical habitats for a wide variety of species. It supports mule deer, white-tailed deer, moose, and species of special concern such as the western gray squirrel. The area also supports numerous birds, including raptors, songbirds, and migratory waterfowl. Streams, riparian zones, and lakes, including Blue Lake, provide important aquatic habitats and serve as key features for recreational fishing. Recent restoration efforts have included tree thinning to create ponderosa pine savanna and improve forest health, riparian restoration, reseeding areas with locally sourced native grasses, and the removal of noxious weeds such as bladder senna and Russian knapweed.

The Sinlahekin Wildlife Area has long been impacted by a history of fire suppression, which has caused forests to become overcrowded with excess fuel, increasing the risk of severe wildfires. Hotter, drier summers, driven by climate change, will further elevate the potential for large wildfires in Washington's eastside forests, compounding the long-standing effects of past fire exclusion and forest management. To address these risks, WDFW developed a prescribed fire program at the Sinlahekin Wildlife Area, marking it as the first wildlife area to reintroduce low-intensity, frequent fire to restore fire-dependent ecosystems.

In the face of increasingly intense and frequent wildfires, WDFW employs a suite of forest management practices to increase the resilience to wildfire and improve forest health across the state. Two of the most critical management tools are forest thinning and prescribed burning. These techniques do more than mitigate the risk of wildfires; they are integral to maintaining the health and resilience of our ecosystems as the climate continues to change.

Thinning, the selective removal of trees and vegetation, is a management practice to decrease forest density, thereby reducing the fuel available for wildfires. Thinning mimics natural disturbances that historically maintained balanced ecosystems by removing trees that are more vulnerable to fire and leaving ones that are most likely to survive the next fire. By carefully managing tree density and species composition, WDFW creates conditions that slow the spread of fire, making it more manageable and less destructive. Thinning also allows more sunlight to reach the forest floor, promoting the growth of diverse plant species that provide essential habitat and food for wildlife. Across Washington's wildlife areas, thinning is not a one-size-fits-all process, but a tailored approach that utilizes both commercial and non-commercial methods to manage forest density and reduce wildfire risk.

Commercial thinning, conducted in partnership with logging companies, involves the removal of trees that can be processed for lumber or paper. This approach not only supports local economies by providing raw materials to mills but also helps maintain healthy forests. The revenue generated from these projects is reinvested into further conservation efforts, creating a cycle of ecological and economic benefit. Non-commercial thinning, meanwhile, targets smaller trees and underbrush with little to no economic value. This labor-intensive technique is often funded by the state Legislature or through grants from conservation partners. Although these projects do not produce immediate economic returns, they play a critical role in forest management by reducing fuel loads, accelerating tree growth, and enhancing the overall health and resilience of the ecosystem.

Prescribed burning is a tool that works in harmony with thinning. By intentionally setting controlled fires under specific conditions, WDFW reduces accumulated vegetation, or "fuel loads," that can contribute to more severe wildfires. These burns mimic natural historical fire cycles in forests through the use of low intensity, low-heat fire to burn off excess fuels and restore quality habitat for wildlife. Prescribed burns rejuvenate the soil, recycle nutrients, and stimulate the growth of fire-adapted species, all while reducing the risk of large, catastrophic fires.

Employing these techniques, the Sinlahekin Ecosystem Restoration Project focused on improving 3,000 acres of fire-dependent habitat in the Sinlahekin Wildlife Area between 2009 and 2016. This project commercially harvested 500 acres, thinning 150 acres by hand, and conducting prescribed burns on 1,350 acres. This work has helped restore ponderosa pine forests to more natural conditions, improve habitat for wildlife like mule deer and bighorn sheep, and reduce the severity of wildfires. In late August of 2015, the treatments were tested by the Lime Belt Fire, which burned through the southern half of the wildlife area. In areas of forest where both thinning and prescribed burning were completed, there was minimal loss of trees to wildfire. But in places that had been thinned, but not yet prescribed burned, most trees were killed by the wildfire. This example shows that thinning and prescribed burning together can be used to reduce wildfire risk and improve forest health.

A prescribed burn in the Sinlahekin Unit of the Sinlahekin Wildlife Area in Okanogan County. Photo credit: WDFW.

Proactive wildfire management, like the practices implemented at the Sinlahekin Wildlife Area, plays a critical role in preserving Washington's diverse ecosystems. These strategies help maintain forest resilience and protect species like the Canada lynx, which relies on high-elevation subalpine and boreal forests to hunt its primary prey, snowshoe hares. Snowshoe hares depend on dense forest cover for survival, but wildfires can destroy this cover, creating a ripple effect that jeopardizes lynx populations. To further support lynx conservation efforts, WDFW personnel, in collaboration with Washington State University, set up camera traps as part of a research project to estimate the abundance of Canada lynx and bobcats in the Sinlahekin Wildlife Area and the nearby Loomis State Forest, providing critical data to inform future management strategies.

Once ranging across northern Washington, lynx are now confined to small areas in western Okanogan, northern Chelan, and parts of Whatcom and Skagit counties. Large-scale wildfires, such as the 2006 Tripod Fire, have caused significant habitat loss, contributing to the species' endangered status in Washington as of 2016. While earlier studies found lynx rarely used the burned areas, recent evidence suggests that regenerating forests in the Tripod Fire area may be providing suitable habitat for lynx and snowshoe hares again, raising cautious optimism about habitat recovery following wildfire.

To better understand this shift, WDFW is collaborating with Home Range Wildlife Research, a non-profit organization in Winthrop that conducts independent and collaborative wildlife research, on a three-year study in the North Cascades. Researchers are using radio collars, trail cameras, and snow tracking to track lynx movements and analyze how they use habitats across different levels of burn severity, vegetation regrowth, and forest fuel levels.

This research seeks to address critical knowledge gaps about lynx habitat use in fire-affected areas and inform forest management strategies to mitigate the impacts of large wildfires while enhancing and preserving lynx habitat in Eastern Washington.

_____

Photos next pages:
(next spread, p. 69) Wildlife Area Manager Bryan Dupont adding grouse to the release pen. These grouse were translocated from southcentral British Columbia to Washington as part of international conservation collaboration efforts between WDFW and British Columbia. Photo Credit: Cari Haug.

(p.70) Sharp-tailed grouse flying out of release pen. This grouse was translocated from southcentral British Columbia to Washington as part of international conservation collaboration efforts between WDFW and British Columbia. Photo Credit: Cari Haug.

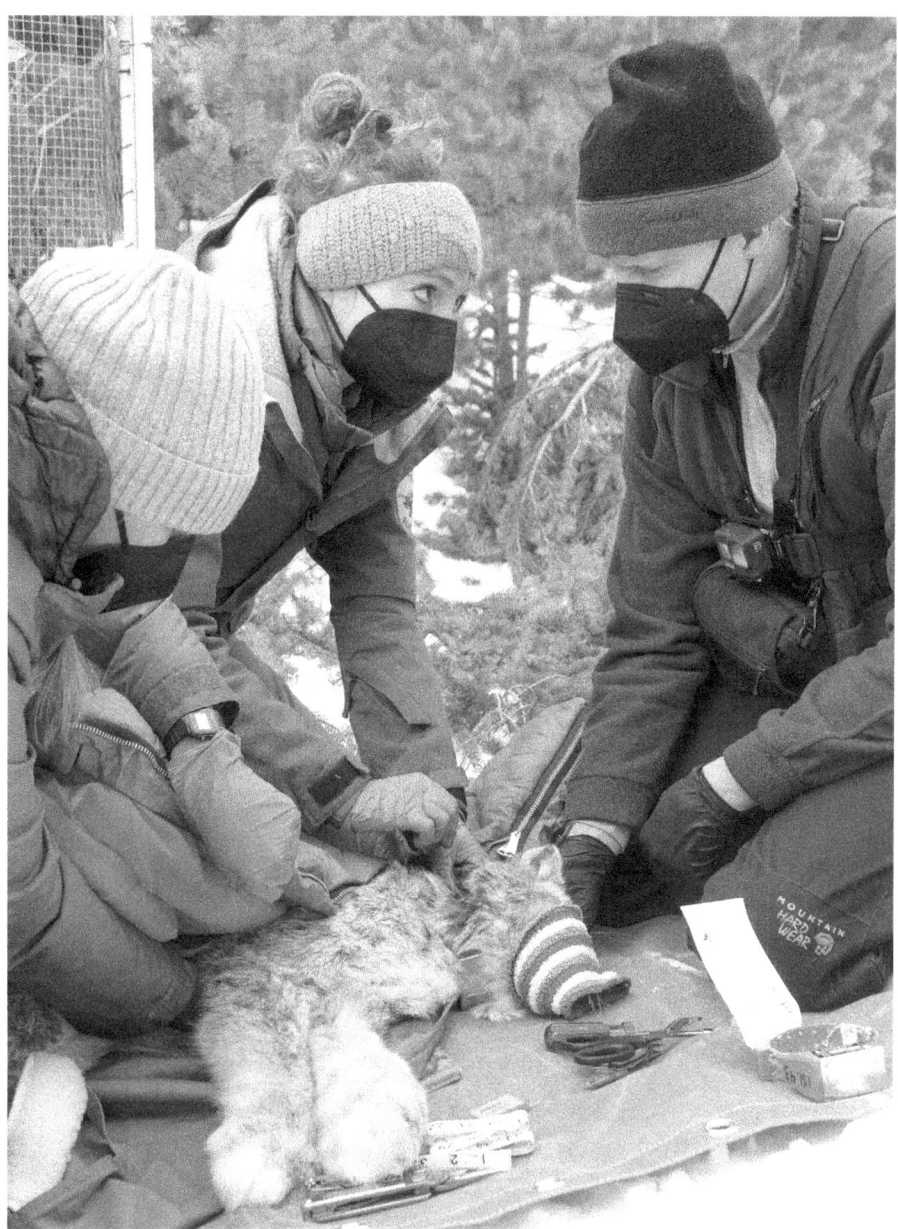

WDFW biologist Scott Fitkin (right) and Home Range Wildlife Research biologists Anna Machocowiz (left) and Carmen Vanbianchi (middle) collar and monitor an immobilized lynx as part of a research project. Photo credit: Christine Phelan.

Sinlahekin Valley and Daughter with Aspen Trees
by Derek Sheffield

Today she lets you lead her down this trail.
Next week she leaves for the rest of her life.
Something has made her laugh.
Probably you as you stop again and scan
the sky for the wings you've never let go of.

This is what you would like to give her,
while we can still see them.
Before she was born, when your life was just you,
you spied the flash of a golden eagle
turning in ever-soaring circles, blue slices of sky

held between the tips of outspread wings.
Above the bare rock of Blue Goat Mountain,
"There," you say as you point. You remember
how her first, fierce cries felt in your arms,
her fiery nakedness and shut eyes.

What will she remember? Will her heart
reach the way an eagle sees, all the way
and always? There's a new cold in the air
gusting down from the Similkameen.
Her steps across gravel fall silent

as a ticking whoosh makes her stop, look up.
Golden leaves blown open, trembling.

Scotch Creek Wildlife Area

The Scotch Creek Wildlife Area spans 26,169 acres across seven units and offers recreational opportunities like hiking, horseback riding, hunting, mountain biking, fishing, and wildlife viewing. Key species include sharp-tailed grouse, mule deer, elk, ruffed grouse, black bear, white-tailed deer, cougars, and upland game birds. Management efforts are focused on habitat restoration, noxious weed control, and infrastructure maintenance to support both wildlife and public access.

The Scotch Creek Unit, the largest unit within the wildlife area, was acquired in 1991 to protect the Columbian sharp-tailed grouse, which was listed by the state as threatened. The unit features critical grassland and shrubsteppe habitats vital for grouse to breed and raise their young. Sharp-tailed grouse rely on special areas called leks, where males gather and perform courtship displays to attract females. Leks are crucial for the sharp-tailed grouse reproduction. When WDFW first acquired the Scotch Creek Unit, only a small population of sharp-tailed grouse remained. Through efforts including shrubsteppe and riparian restoration, along with bird translocations from other states and Canada, the population was recovering. By spring 2015, the Scotch Creek Unit reached a peak of 116 birds across four active lek sites, representing a major conservation success.

However, progress was severely impacted later that year when the 2015 Okanogan Complex fire, one of the largest wildfires in state history, swept through the region, destroying all lek sites on the Scotch Creek and Tunk Valley Units. The wildfire damaged critical summer and winter grouse habitat, leaving the population highly vulnerable. Despite this devastation, some unburned patches, particularly areas with birch trees, provided refuge for surviving grouse. The fire underscored the fragility of the species and the urgent need for continued restoration efforts to ensure habitat resilience against future wildfire.

In 2018, the state listed the sharp-tailed grouse as endangered, prompting WDFW to intensify conservation efforts. Building on this urgency, WDFW partnered with the British Columbia Ministry of Forests, Lands, Natural Resource Operations and Rural Development to translocate dozens of sharp-tailed grouse from healthy populations in British Columbia to Scotch Creek, tribal lands, and adjacent private lands in Tunk Valley. These birds, evenly divided between males and females, were assessed for health; some were equipped with monitoring transmitters and released into the wildlife area. This translocation aimed to stabilize the sharp-tailed grouse population, which had dropped to fewer than 1,000 individuals statewide due to habitat loss. The project was made possible through funding from the National Fish and Wildlife Foundation, Pittman-Robertson funds, and state resources, with significant support from partners such as the Colville Confederated Tribes, Douglas County PUD, and private landowners. This collaborative effort highlights the importance of partnerships in restoring threatened species and reflects ongoing dedication to rebuilding the sharp-tailed grouse population in Washington.

Translocations have become a critical tool for sharp-tailed grouse recovery, particularly as climate change and increasing wildfire risks threaten the resilience of their habitat. By relocating birds from healthier populations, WDFW and its partners aim to bolster local populations and enhance genetic diversity. These efforts, combined with habitat restoration and collaboration with stakeholders, are essential to safeguarding the species against mounting environmental pressures and ensuring the long-term survival of the sharp-tailed grouse in Washington.

On a Trail Like This
by Jill McCabe Johnson

I learned to read on a trail
like this.
   I measured the seasons
watching spikelets and bracts
of northwestern sedge turn purple
in spring before fruiting into summer's
seeds.
   I scanned the ground
for clusters of horned larks who've
burrowed nests in these lands
since the early Pleistocene.
      Quaking
aspen rustled a whispery backdrop
to lark chirp and trills and in winter
made sugar from sunlight
bathing its silvery bark.
     Charcoal
stains wisped up the trunks
of ponderosa pine, a reminder
of flash fires thrashing through
their stands.
   Some days, dense
patches of fog camouflaged
mourning dove and quail who shun
the pinpoint gaze of cooper's
hawks.
   Today, when serviceberries
have already blushed their deepest
indigo, I sweep my eyes hoping
to glimpse the white-tailed jackrabbits
once more before winter sets in.

Sharp-Tailed and Shimmering
by Jill McCabe Johnson

It's not easy to spot grouse
in the first dusting of snowfall
amid autumn's golden grasses.

A herd of elk lows in the distance
as the male grouse shudder tail feathers
and dance in the lek—mating ground

where they flash purplish balloons
at the sides of their necks to impress
females who will brood in their clutches.

Wintered down at creek's edge
food is scarce in the ruinous
remnants of wildfire

yet stands of water birch harbor
hatchlings with their beaks agape
not quite ready to take flight.

By the season of bitterroot
yarrow and pearly everlasting,
the grouse forage in shrubsteppe,

camouflaged by sedges and wheatgrass
that release seeds and indecipherable secrets
whispered under evening winds.

Paper wasps etch trails on fallen
lodgepole pine and construct
their mâchéd castles. Cougars pad behind

the winding scent of white-tailed deer
while black bears dream of salmon leaping
toward their natal streams come spring.

Our Common Fate
by Roger William Gilman

> *. . . and yet, when we reach the abyss between us, we remain almost all the way*
> *to each other.* —Paul Celan, *The Meridian*

One

> *The bodies and brains of creatures from which we have evolved are often*
> *simpler versions of ourselves. Find the zoo inside you.* —Neil Shubin, *Your Inner Fish*

The Skagit River rumbles and spits below us
as you and I stand above this troubled water and watch an eagle
watching a salmon swim upstream at the end of its life.
This ancient green steel-frame bridge crosses the river just north of its
confluence with Cascade Creek—itself a river by now, an influence.
It's a moment joining the four of us eye to eye with the river that
runs through this space and time—through Marblemount, Millers Point,
Sedro Woolley, La Conner, Deception Pass, and out in the Salish Sea.

This fresh water has dribbled from a headwater glacier, been
aerated by noisy cascades of logs and boulders before it runs
out quick and quiet on a flat farming plain, snaking the lowland
and channeling saltmarsh before it embraces a great vastness in the
North Pacific: from constrained trickle to wide openness, from
sparkling light to a darkened deep, from sweet to salty water.
And then the turn: giddy-eyed smolts, returning as sea-run veterans
with old isinglass eyes and a longing lately grown up.

The well-seasoned river is shallow and braided today just
around the bend down-valley from here, now that last year's floods have
disbanded. Its series of gravel-bars puncture and stich the boundary
between air and water, and separate upper from lower reaches of the
river. It's a transitional moment for all the bodies and brains that once
floated downstream away from home—away from here. A developmental
place in which one could grow up, and not just older; a distinction our
parents seem to insist on.

Upriver east of here, toward the snow and ice of Eldorado Peak, past
native villages, beyond Settler dams and powerplants, far into the high

country of glaciers, comes a hundred-thousand trickles, out of Inspiration
Ice Fields—braiding themselves into creeks soon to be swallowed by
this hungry river rushing headlong downhill against all the artificial light
and darkness we've created for our cousin salmons. Oh, the risk of it
all—the terrible journey, measured not only by distance and duration,
but by destination and death.

As we stand here on the high bridge, we swear we'll return another
day and sing a new batch of sea-bright salmon home from the sea—
as generations of fisher men and women have before us. We're
all fishers now. But we must not fish these fish: the warming climate
of our lives, and theirs, claims too many babies, theirs and ours.
And so, we'll save the fish for themselves—those great value-holders
other than ourselves: without salmon we'd sing only to ourselves—as if
such art was never meant for others.

At a big bend further downstream, the river cuts into its corner,
digging a deeper curve that reveals even more of the tangled bank,
the condition of our lives—eagle, salmon, human, and all other six
and four and two legged ones: the feathered and finned, the furred,
scaled, and barked, even the thin-skinned ones—all this wealth of
the entangling bank. The running, swimming, flying, crawling, rooting
and walking ones—all the structure and function of each other's lives—
making the tangle more connected and interactive; inter-dependent.

Such knowledge is a map. But the map is not the territory. The Skagit
defines its territory as a great watershed of tributaries storing energy
in everything that lives from its flowing—dependent entanglements
constantly adjusting to each other, cooperatively competing
for each other's energy—giving and taking—each a conduit
to all the others in the web; the muskrat on a tide-flat eating clams,
a sockeye salmon grabbing caddisflies from thin air, an eagle with
a fist-full of fishhooks dive-bombing the river for lunch.

Ask the river about the layers of fact and value, relations of events and
processes that are as meaningful to one life-form as to another—the
world-wide web of life entangling and enabling us all—by attraction and
curiosity, with hunger and fear. It will advise our saving it to save the rest

of the tangled bank—and thereby save our own souls. The journey out and back is a circle that must not be broken: from glacier trickle to creek tumble and river flow, from sea currents of real consequence, then evaporation and return. Clouds hovering over home. The rain.

This view from the bridge is not a view from nowhere—as if we could stand outside space and time; it's a member's view, a local perspective on a place and moment in the only world we have. Like all situated-seeing, our observations include objects of concern that confront us with questions about duties that creatures such as we might have toward the rest of nature—those with eyes and faces not so unlike our own that ask us for community and solidarity, compassion and kindness, dignity and respect.

All types of creatures, great and small, acquire great value from small roles they play in this entangled web of life—in time and the river—a value added to that of life itself. Our common fate is shared moments in a shared watershed—in the shared circuitry of living. We celebrate this inter-dependence, diversity of role players, and value of this expensive journey we endeavor together.
The river corridor we migrate carries the evolved wisdom of salmon—the embodiment of connection and conversation, the dependence and reciprocity of forest and valley, and open sea.

We rehearse our shared life as fish and fishers—celebrate our shared journey traveling from gravel-nest and home-stream near the cliff-end of a mountain glacier; we glory in our downhill float away from home, into a wide sophisticated sea where only too soon we'll turn and swim back up that river we've already ventured—now bearing gifts of salty nutrient—nitrogen, carbon, and phosphorous—all the way home to our headwaters, hoping to find water cold and clean enough to birth babies and to ease a simple death.

Two
We depend on salmon; they depend on us. —Billy Frank, *NW Indian Fisheries Newsletter*

Remember how we began as eggs? tailor-made for our own water in a mountain meadow's shallow stream, in our parent's gravel nest, where we were washed tenderly by clean water? How we began as rose-colored

pearls coded for some kind of life worth living and waiting for that good
gelatinous coverlet of milt? And remember how quickly we blossomed
forth as infant alevins, eager to become toddler fingerling-fry? So
translucent and soft, so ill-formed and unruly? Forest animals already
imprinting scents of minerals in the homestead: bread baking,
cut grass, fallen apples, wood smoke.

Mom and Dad chose well, didn't they: coarse-enough cobble to allow
Continuous flows of cold oxygen-rich water—and a redd dug deep
enough to protect their treasure from being flushed downstream before it
even hatched. We stayed the winter near home, three-or-four months,
swallowing plankton. Then in spring, as parrs, we munched on stoneflies,
mayflies, caddisflies, and on midges carried by the flow while we explored
the refuge of side-channels in our stream. Before long we were exploring
gurgling riffles and roaring cascades of
the big-bouldered and logged-clogged creek ahead.

All too soon we're schooled into pre-teen parr groups, eager to be leaving
home as teenage smolts, dressing in silver sequins that will replace the
dowdy, mud-colored camouflage of spots-and-bars our parents gave us:
new fashion more appropriate to the fast life and bright lights of a big-city
salty sea, far away from home. And now, our journey underway, we sluice
down noisy falling water and float awkwardly toward a wide
cosmopolitan sea of mixed-stock schools of fish. Smoltification allows
us to survive salty water and tells us, without parenting,
to release ourselves to a world of friends

and enemies. Those who leave their birthplace and comfort zone for a
rough and tumble life abroad, inevitably come home energized and
humbled, wiser—ready to restore and reactivate their native stream.
Because our flesh will be torn and taste of salt and oil, we'll be eager to
get home and produce a hardy generation of children or disciples—
with as much hope and curiosity as the last one. As smolts we're
neither proper nor improper being—just raw potential—running
the river away from home, memorizing every twist and turn
we take, already rehearsing our way home: memorizing

the sights and smells of everything coming into view as we slide

downhill—the scent of mother's redd and the krill we ate as fry; the
watermelon algae, spring-blown pollen, and ice worms of the glacier;
the scent of gravel, the perfumes of heather and mushroom along the
tangled corridor. This complex scent includes odors of cedar, basalt
and iron-tailings, rot of beaver-felled logs and the spray of skunk; musk
of willow-leaf fermenting in the swamp, a fisherman's cold-coffee
leftovers, juice of seeping skunk-cabbage
dripping from an onshore bog,

fragrance of fresh raindrops off mint leaves in the ditch, rhododendron
petal and huckleberry tea, the mist of moist moss and fern.
It's a sequence well worth remembering; and so, we continue catching
hints of the river—at the place of hatch-and-swarming caddisflies;
capturing whiffs of last year's fish heads,
odors of leather hiking-boots and rubber waders. We begin numbering
tributaries, bridges and culverts, patches of mosquitos and gnats,
mudslides of otter bellies. We detect aromas of lost sandwiches in
picnic parks on the bluff, pungent odors of creosote railroad ties and

asphalt of country roads. And Wow! the sweet smell of kernel corn
and apple orchard; then a reek of careless cow manure and stink of
insect pesticide; traces of tulips near Fishtown, a leaching garbage dump,
burnt tractor tires, pungent canneries and breweries, the barnacled
bottoms of fishing boats, musk of muskrat, crap of dog-run, guano of
seagull stuck on roofs of derelict barns, musty cattails in the salt marsh,
eelgrass blades covered with nudibranch snails, the scent
of kelp, and growing density of salt in the tide-flat: all of this,
before we plunge waves and begin rafting crazy currents

in Deception Pass and finally abandon ourselves to lure of ports that
rim the Salish Sea. Ready to become sea-run salmon, we've already seen
a lot on our way here—even if seeing it only in our own image. We'll
soon be ready to surrender this Self to duties of memory and prepare
to teach a next generation how to survive and flourish in growing heat,
the scorch and boil—how to swim deeper and to trick those
who stoke wildfire, teach how to forgive one's mother and father who
thought they did their best. Soon we'll be ready to move beyond
standing face-to-face and turn toward a future working side-by-side.

Three

There's a point on every trail, given time of day and weather, that's turn-around time.
—David Guterson, *Turn Around Time*

At sea, during the roaming years as silver-sided sea-run salmon, we gang
with the school, bulk-up body and brain, ripen lateral-lines either side of
our newly buffed and torpedoed bodies, the better to orient a point of
view on distance and direction, vibration and pressure—on surrounding
predators and prey . . . the better to school with our redd mates and
navigate currents in the vastness, hunting a local food and happiness,
with hope of one day heading home and evading all those
dead intimations of mortality floating limp and empty downhill,
passed us to the nearest snag.

In a great grazing ground of the North Pacific—dodging orcas, sharks
and seals, and practicing swimming against the current—we ready
ourselves for the challenge of ending where we began. We'll learn fin
and twist-tail. Under clouds of pain and fear we begin remembering
comforts of home—the feel of cold sweet water washing through our
gills in a shallow sunlit stream without any trace of darkness of the
deep. We suddenly remember moral simplicities of eating food that
doesn't painfully anticipate its capture and that avoids humiliation
of hanging by one's jaw from some indecent finger.

Hormones shift and we feel the call of our homestead (or is it the sex),
imagining the scent of our home river—of mother's gravel nest
and father's musk—partners ready to make babies or disciples.
It's turn-around time! We shift from eyes and ears to nares and let a
beautiful mix of stored-up smells guide us home. The scent of the world
has finally found and held us for this moment. It's not that we're worn
or weary, or the current has gotten dark and cold, but that we've stood
too long passively waiting to be salvaged from gutters and back alleys
of the deep. Only now do we really remember family and friends,

begin longing for the old neighborhood and making an active turn
toward home. We know the home we'll find won't be the one we've left.
But summoned by tides, we funnel into the throat of our river to begin
the ascent toward home—an adventure in itself—ready to fuel the future.

Waiting in the wetland mouth of our river we catch an incoming wave and surf to the first rapid requiring a mighty twist of tail and leap of faith —our river-provoked power. Each ethnic group of salmon in its turn heads upriver toward high-country to find its special stream and final work as Mariners and Mountaineers. We're all salmon people now.

Heading upriver from Miller's Point, to where the downhill rush of water finds the inflection-point of its angle of repose—the flatland now behind us west to the Samish Flats and Salish Sea—we begin leaping that narrow water we once slid down. As salmons we pause in pools and gather strength for the next rush and lunge that employs painful tail-twists and long leaps, as we power toward a home we haven't seen in years, persistent hormones driving a desire to spawn, even in the absence of hope of seeing, let alone ever really knowing, our young. We slog on.

We take the turn into Cascade Creek leading toward our old neighborhood below the Inspiration Ice Fields on broken-toothed knife-edged Eldorado Peak. Adopting a flint-face we resolve to begin again—the battering, the leaping and scraping, the backsliding. We persist against the grain of bright rushing, noisy wate—with all the sights and scents of home pulling us upward and forward, transforming us, yet again. We muscle our way to higher ground, our bashed and gashed flesh exposed to a gauntlet of hungry eagles, otters, and bears. And gillnetters. Willing to risk it all for ascendence.

We gamble our precious cargo of fresh eggs and milt for this calling that Will consume us. Soon we'll be meat-and-bone fertilizer in the tangled bank, as our final autumn turns winter, and we die into some future or other. As travel companions nearing home, we put on breeding colors— burn crimson and blossom green—capacities for love and death. At our special stream one of us catches the eye of the other and starts nosing around the lateral-lines, causing a ruckus, thrashing and quivering, hovering with joy and fear, ready to release a bloated belly full of pearls into a bed that wants that plain quilt of milt.

Nearing home, we see brothers and sisters—their expiration dates passed – side-tilting or back-floating without energy or agency, drifting

downhill or already stuck in the verge, begging to be fertilizer.
Only if the eggs will not boil, and if fear and hunger or affection
produce a kinship that animalizes humans and personifies salmons will
we narrow the empathy and solidarity gap that terrifies us, natives and
settlers alike. The moral meaning of dependence in a scorching world
creates a duty to provide each other shelter—local trees that shade and
cool local wate—a duty to meet expectations of the tangled bank.

It hits me how finite and fragile a courage it takes to be faithful to my
future—to care for something larger and more valuable than difference
—committed to the principle that life is life, and love is love. This is
truth naturalized: the tangled bank creating duties of allegiance and
care-taking—to local reform and restoration, to clean, local free-flowing
water and everything that lives because of it. My world is built of local
things; local relations, viewed from local places and moments.
Everything I inherit is first a local thing. I'm locally endangered; locally
protected. Should I not save unbroken my local circle of life.

Four
  There is no morality without metaphorical imagination. —Paul Ricoeur, *Oneself as Another*

We've returned to the bridge at Millers Point, several years after watching
smolts pour downstream, now returned transformed
and more conscious of entanglements. We raise binoculars
just in time to see an eagle swoop from its cottonwood perch,
talons extending forward from her body
as she nears the water like a baseball runner sliding feet-first
into second base. The river's skin tears open as our fish-eagle muscles
its way up and out of a cold current with a dripping salmon
whose face is as terrified as ours is horrified.

We've returned to the bridge to see more than what returns; we're here
to imagine ourselves as something else—a human salmonized, a salmon
personalized. Such shapeshifting—metaphorical, not metaphysical—is
no escape from reality but a going deeper into natures and conditions
of what we share: evolutionary history, ecological forces, the watershed
and river, a journey with hard U-turn and fraught future. Every analogy
has its disanalogy: only one species is eventually responsible

for the river—for abating its pollution, deoxygenation,
its warming, damming and draining,

its over-harvest. And repair. Every creature has right to habitat it needs
for developing and exercising its species-specific capacities.
I ask the River. It tells me to "join a land and water trust" that
voluntarily protects and promotes the tangled bank.
It tells me "Don't just stand there on the bridge complaining
'Oh, it was all once so beautiful' or glibly wade into the water
and cast some cheap poetic line and artificial fly for a sporting game
of 'catch and release'." I covenant clearly now with my entanglements:
Save what depends on me. Everything needs saving sometimes.

The question in the eye of the salmon that catches my eye now is not
"Do you understand me?" But "How will you treat me?" At this
confluence of rivers, from where the sun now stands, I swear to accept
my duty of care for what, in the past, I saw as having a duty to sustain
me; I resolve to repair what I've damaged and diminished. I resolve to
become haunted by the River and everything that lives
because of its flowing. I hear the salmons in my river tell me
to go home after my great adventure, and to make sure
my compass is as moral as it is magnetic.

I'll tell others what I've learned of my salmon nature: Go with the flow
until it's imperative to resist; Join a school and know where you're
going; Head straight into the fray and start ascending, hurtling any
obstacle. Share food and shelter. Make a hard turn when you run out of
luck, and Trust you'll find a way home. Become the water,
land and forest. Take only what is given and what you need. Commit to
the ultimate act of keeping it all going-on. Show gratitude to all the
species that make your life possible. Acknowledge that it's a gift
to share responsibility for nurturing and preserving all its life and talent.

And now, with all the present intimations of your mortality
floating downstream, let the River ask you What you should make of
your one and only, short and dangerous, Life.

WEST CASCADES ECOREGION

L.T. Murray Wildlife Area
Poet Joseph Powell

West Cascades Ecoregion

The West Cascades Ecoregion in Washington extends from just east of the Cascade Mountains' summit to the foothills of the Puget Lowland, spanning from Snoqualmie Pass southward to the Columbia River Gorge. The topography and soils of the West Cascades have been profoundly shaped by its volcanic history. This mountain range is home to several prominent volcanoes, including Mount Rainier and Mount St. Helens, both of which define much of the region's ecology. Alpine glaciation has influenced the landscape, though alpine and subalpine habitats are less extensive than in the North Cascades ecoregion.

Characterized by a wet, mild climate, the West Cascades receive between 55 and 140 inches of annual precipitation, with snowpack at higher elevations providing critical water resources. Conifer forests dominate the landscape. Below 4,000 feet, Douglas fir is the most common tree, often growing alongside western hemlock. At higher elevations, Pacific silver fir, mountain hemlock, and subalpine fir become more dominant. Other conifers such as western redcedar, grand fir, and noble fir are also common throughout the region. Above 7,000 feet, harsh conditions prevent tree growth, giving way to alpine meadows, low shrubs, wetlands, and areas of bare rock and ice. Throughout the ecoregion, habitats such as riparian zones, grassy balds—unique, treeless meadows typically found on ridges or mountain summits—and wetlands host a rich diversity of plants and wildlife, including endemic species found near Mount Rainier and in the Columbia River Gorge. The ecoregion is also home to unique species, such as the Cascade torrent salamander and bull trout, which depend on cold, fast-moving streams, and iconic species like the northern spotted owl and marbled murrelet that thrive in old-growth forests.

Climate change is altering hydrology and habitat conditions for wildlife in the West Cascade Ecoregion. More precipitation is falling as rain instead of snow, reducing snowpack and leading to earlier spring runoff. This shift affects streamflows and water availability in summer, stressing cold-water species like salmon, steelhead, and bull trout. Warmer temperatures are also increasing the frequency of wildfires, especially in areas where fire suppression has led to dense forests with heavy fuel loads. These shifts are altering habitat conditions, and in response many species will need to shift their ranges or move across the landscape to track suitable habitat and resources.

With the majority of this ecoregion under public ownership, the West Cascades Ecoregion remains a critical area for conservation, recreation, and ecological resilience.

L.T. Murray Wildlife Area

The L.T. Murray Wildlife Area in Kittitas County spans approximately 118,300 acres across five units, interspersed with lands managed by the Department of Natural Resources, Bureau of Land Management, and the U.S. Forest Service in a checkerboard pattern. This wildlife area plays a vital role in protecting critical winter range for deer and elk, with around 2,000 elk fed each winter to minimize damage to private agricultural lands. From mid-December to mid-March, hay is distributed daily at two feeding sites, providing popular elk viewing and educational opportunities. The area also safeguards upland game bird habitat, sage grouse habitat, and endangered steelhead fisheries. Active habitat management includes controlling weeds on 600-1,000 acres annually, reseeding with native vegetation when feasible, and collaborating with the Kittitas County Noxious Weed Control Board.

The wildlife area offers diverse recreational opportunities, such as hunting, camping, fishing, wildlife viewing, off-road vehicle (ORV) and snowmobile riding, horseback and bicycle riding, and hiking. Recently, activities like bird watching, shed antler collection, and ORV riding have grown in popularity. Through active management and habitat restoration, the L.T. Murray Wildlife Area serves as a steward of Washington's natural resources, preserving lands and waters for the benefit of both people and wildlife.

The Yakima River Unit, part of the L.T. Murray Wildlife Area, spans 2,668 acres of diverse habitat in Kittitas County along the Yakima River. The largest property lies south of the river in the eastern foothills of the Central Cascades, including Cabin and Cole creeks, with uplands dominated by coniferous forests. These lands are managed primarily for federal and state-listed species and other species of concern. The Yakima River supports a variety of fish, including summer steelhead, spring and summer Chinook, bull trout, rainbow trout, west slope cutthroat trout, mountain whitefish, and nonnative brook and brown trout. This unit plays a crucial role in the recovery of bull trout, a priority for WDFW.

Adjacent to Lake Easton State Park and the Palouse to Cascades State Trail, the area offers recreational opportunities such as hiking, hunting, wildlife viewing, fishing, and winter activities like cross-country skiing and snowshoeing. Recent additions, such as the Teanaway Junction Boat Launch with primitive amenities, have further enhanced river access for fishing and boating.

An aerial photo of the wildlife overcrossing at the Snoqualmie Pass East Project on I-90 near Snoqualmie Pass, Washington, where heavy traffic creates a barrier to wildlife. Increasing connectivity is one of the most frequently recommended adaptation strategies for biodiversity management in a changing climate. Photo credit: WSDOT.

The Yakima River Unit, the northern border of which abuts Interstate 90 (I-90), is a vital component of efforts to reconnect fragmented landscapes and enhance habitat connectivity in the Cascade Range. Habitat connectivity refers to the permeability of natural landscapes that allows wildlife to move freely in search of food, mates, and, in a changing climate, more suitable habitats. As air temperatures rise, many species are shifting their ranges to cooler northern latitudes or higher elevations, but their movements are often obstructed by human-made barriers such as highways, urban sprawl, and agricultural lands. For wide-ranging species like elk, black bears, and mountain lions, as well as smaller, less mobile species like turtles and amphibians, these barriers can fragment critical habitats.

I-90, a major transportation corridor, exemplifies this challenge, dividing high-quality habitats in the Cascades and creating a dangerous obstacle for wildlife. Roadway connectivity is a crucial element of habitat connectivity, as highways pose not only physical barriers but also risks of wildlife-vehicle collisions, endangering both animals and motorists. To address these challenges, the Washington State Department of Transportation, in partnership with WDFW and Conservation Northwest, initiated the I-90 Snoqualmie Pass East Project. This effort, which includes wildlife crossing structures like the nationally recognized I-90 Wildlife Overcrossing, reconnects habitats bisected by the highway. Designed to support species such as cougar, black bear, moose, lynx, and wolverine, the overpass—along with underpasses and fencing—enables safe wildlife movement, reduces collisions, and restores ecological connectivity across the north and south Cascades.

The Yakima River Unit contributes to these efforts by providing protected lands adjacent to the highway that enhance connectivity for wildlife. By acting as a critical link in a broader network of habitats, the unit helps support the safe migration and range shifts needed for species to adapt to a warming climate. This role underscores the importance of integrating landscape conservation with road mitigation efforts to create a more permeable and resilient environment for wildlife.

Looking beyond the I-90 corridor, WDFW and WSDOT are advancing habitat connectivity statewide through the Washington Wildlife Habitat Connectivity Action Plan. Completed in 2025, this comprehensive strategy identifies high-priority connectivity areas and actionable steps to protect and expand these corridors. Initiatives include developing wildlife crossing structures, implementing wildlife-friendly fencing, and using spatial tools to help local jurisdictions incorporate connectivity into land-use planning. By addressing connectivity challenges at both the local and statewide levels, this plan aims to preserve Washington's biodiversity and enable wildlife to thrive amid ongoing climate and habitat changes. Together, efforts like these and the Yakima River Unit's contributions form a cornerstone of Washington's commitment to fostering a resilient ecological network.

Cabin Creek running through the Yakima Unit of L.T. Murray Wildlife Area.
Photo credit: Alan Bauer.

The Yakima River
by Joseph Powell

1.

At ten I splashed its flanks for fish,
saw its world of otters, beavers, minks,
those slinky divers, water's weavers;
garter snakes afloat or essing with ease;
herons doing Tai Chi, or still as stones,
poised to throw their one spear;
clouds drinking; black-masked ospreys dragging their tiny
reflections until their prey rises
and they dive to meet themselves, that empty handshake,
and emerge, dripping, shaking themselves
already looking toward the next graspable thing.

Turned over rocks for their teeming
underbellies, that squiggle of nymphs
crawling toward wings; underwater worms;
feisty crawdads shaking their fat fists;
ridged mussel shells, purple-streaked pearl,
flashing white under the riffles;
blotched and spiny sculpins moving their great fans,
their big heads almost half their bodies,
little philosophers under their chosen stones.
The glitter of skwalas, mayflies, midges,
gray-drakes, and olive duns,
mica of the air, this water's deft dreaming;
waxwings weaving their parabolas,
collecting these sunlit minutes.

Saw shoreline cottonwoods ringed by studious mouths,
standing like pencils on their fat pieces of lead,
chips scattered like shavings,
wondering which direction falling takes,
fifty years of innerness open as a newspaper.

Felt water's pushing onrushing weight

like a thousand invisible hands
in a crowd of oblivious hurry,
how its heavy surges swamp
inner sovereignty, ridicule dawdling,
on-and-on its mantra,
as it falls toward always.

                    2.

Young I swam full-strength against its on-rushing
side currents, going almost nowhere,
but loving the tensile pressure,
that wet equilibrium, that poise of power.
Now I drift with it, letting it take me,
swimming without swimming, earth-flying,
feeling each swale and hesitation, each swirl
and swift plunge, bobbing like an apple,
time's fruit, its lineage and language.
I'm of it, its object, its eye,
bobbing over and into eons,
that cyclic permanence inside each bead,
that droplet I am and am becoming.

Clarity is its milieu, moves how the mind moves
from burnished thing to thing, until something vital
rises out of it, a depth exposed, thus preyable.
It moves as it meditates, its eddies downward spirals,
motion's obsession, a gyre, released as undertow,
censuring the smooth sailing of its surface.
When I stare into this moving mirror,
it stares into me. Again looking up
the world changes, swivels on changing air—
trees sway away from their trunks,
snags reach for their missing leaves,
grasses ascend sagebrush hills
and return on rolling waves of light.

It's a way of being, a wandering force,
gathering in its minions—Taneum, Naneum, Manastash,

Ahtanum, Toppenish, Satus,. . .--,
its lesser rivers, Cle Elum, Teanaway, Naches—
tucking them in like a hen its chicks.
It swells or diminishes, stalls or plunges,
bends to assess and embrace, bathes what it destroys,
births what it beats, polishes edges, floats or sinks what's foreign,
mutters to itself, leans into farmers' Wilson Creek silt and poisons,
runoff, washes away foam and Styrofoam, cans and bottles,
rusts cars and carts, rods and rims, flashes its plastics
like the glitter of strippers, but always pushing forward,
its nine million year old speech.

L.T. Murray Wildlife Unit
by Joseph Powell

1.

We come with cameras now to show
the land we love is ours, in light and shadow,

that being here will verify we're happy,
wandering from ourselves like willful refugees.

Rainier stands up stark above the hills,
in its skirt of snow and pale blue veils,

proving, for once, how clear our distances,
how some beauty stands at the end of our vacancies,

how mysteriously the shifting plates advance,
how vast our upper and underworlds, how appearance

can draw us into such spectacular realms,
despite the inhospitable facts and systems.

The hilltop artful curving waves of evergreens
receding to sage are like throws on davenos;

the lava runs of lichened rock are like old maps
of land in Bleau's beige ocean, legend-wrapped.

Our ancestors walked or rode these hills,
marveling, too, at the stretch of visible miles,

usually passing, like us, without truly seeing
that intertexture of terranean life, that teeming

bareness we walk through—rattlers, larks,
talking sage, fungal fugues, lizards stalking ants, monarchs,

the mumbling buzz of bees, stink beetle handstands,
the band of blood-thirsty ticks alert on sage fronds,

the air-march of web-sailing spiders, head-bobbing
bluebellies, bite-mad gadflies, northern blues closing/opening,

and underfoot the seeds and roots of violets, yellow bells,
bitterroot, mariposa, delicacies so deft they mind-swell.

Millenia of moccasin-prints, agate arrowheads, bird-points,
scrapers, knives, stretch toward time's vanishing point.

2.

—*Pinus ponderosa: bull, blackjack, western yellow, filpinus, ponderos*
—*Stan Kitchen sampled a ponderosa pine in Utah that was 933 years old*

Across the arid steppe, the ponderosas
find their niches, and through inchling growth,
as if in league with timelessness,
rise like grand candles in a green flame.
At 250 feet, the tallest desert lookouts,
they are the bland eye's colored map pins,
definition's balance, delusion's confusion;
their green, too, is the eye's rest, its bounty.
Self-walled from fire by puzzle-pieces
of bark overlaid and overlaid until they scatter
and collect in middens at the base.
Their black seams run like mudcracks in creekbeds.
Their sunned resin, sweet as fresh pipe tobacco.

But after years of stark summer dryness,
the toxic exhaust of moving nations,
the Cow and Evans Canyon Fires burned
these green oases into darkened haunted spaces.
Hundreds of years of growth and green now
charred corpses in cartoon graveyards,
bare branches with nothing to reach for,
cottonwoods and chokecherries also soot sentinels,
dissolving faster than ascent,
bark loosening and falling, limbs withered and brittle.

Only birds and avid burrowers and sunken bulbs
found the shape of escape—the sizzling scorch
and hushed rush of fire turning everything
to dust until our boots print in black snow
and any food's miles away. Singed beer cans,
melted glass, wire, bent metal posts and bands,
destruction's relics, how we lay waste.

3.

lewisii rediviva, racine amer

Bitterroot can live a year without water,
rise up through its own ashes,
the *resurrection flower*, and bloom like pale pink loti
in pools of dust and clumps of basalt,
their ruddy leafless pods burst into petals
like star-scatter across dirt skies.
The Shoshone-Bannock boiled
and pounded them, added meat and berries.
Lewis found these roots "nauseating."
Their shine is of beauty's bitterness.

4.

In any vista is the history of eyes
set on finding a path, forward or away;
behind each shadow are a thousand shadows,
days without end, marking time in their
timeless way; the angle of any vision
sees much more than it can comprehend;
purpose puts all else on the periphery,
that tree, that canyon green with trees,
that bare hill, that wide expanse of blackened sage,
are singular, part of a stratagem, a journey,
some plotting of distance, lunch, nightfall;
and more quickly than we pass, they recede,
memory's background, toys of time and design,

destination's mileage, the blue-black haze of hindsight.
These trees, hundreds of years old, belonged to others,
to personal histories, eras of violence, of hatreds,
of peace; they breathed in our exhalations,
were totems and blazed boundaries,
goals and disappointments.
Like blackened cities, they'll mount the air
ahead of us, as they did behind, casting their seeds
into a present now long into our futures.

EAST CASCADES ECOREGION

East Cascades Ecoregion
Poet Catalina Marie Cantú

∽

Wenas Wildlife Area
Poet DJ Lee

∽

Klickitat Wildlife Area
Poet Jim Cantú

East Cascades Ecoregion

The East Cascades Ecoregion of Washington extends from just east of the Cascade Crest, stretching from Cle Elum south to the Columbia River Gorge. This region experiences a more continental climate than the wetter ecoregions to the west, with greater temperature extremes, warm, dry summers, and cold winters. Precipitation levels vary widely due to changes in elevation and latitude, with the higher peaks receiving significantly more moisture than the lower, drier foothills.

Vegetation in the East Cascades is shaped by these climatic and elevational gradients. Open forests of ponderosa pine and lodgepole pine dominate the lower elevations, while Douglas fir and other fir species like grand fir and white fir become more common at higher altitudes. Closer to the Cascade Crest, wetter conditions support fir and hemlock forests, while shrubsteppe and grasslands characterize the easternmost, arid portions of the ecoregion. This vegetation is adapted to the region's dry conditions but is highly vulnerable to wildfire.

As a transition zone between the wetter forests west of the Cascade Crest and the drier Columbia Plateau, the Eastern Cascade Ecoregion is especially sensitive to climate change impacts. Similar to eastside forests in the North Cascades, this ecoregion is expected to experience hotter, drier summers, reduced snowpack, and earlier declines in soil moisture, increasing drought stress on vegetation and reducing water availability. The historical role of frequent, low-severity fires in shaping these forests has been disrupted by nearly a century of fire suppression, leading to denser forests and greater fuel loads. These conditions, compounded by warmer temperatures and drier summer conditions, heighten the risk of large, high-severity wildfires, which threaten forest resilience, wildlife habitats, and local communities.

Ecology Haiku
by Catalina Marie Cantú

Cascades rain shadow

hawk dives for squirrel meal

wheatgrass smoldering.

Northern sagebrush lizard basking in the sun at the Wenas Wildlife Area. Photo credit: Melinda Gray.

The Flying Cross
by Catalina Marie Cantú

I lift my bluish-gray broad rounded wings and shake my long-barred white tail. My pale body with "rufous barring" nestles over my six bluish-white spotted eggs. Six! Not our usual three or four. My mate and I protected our eggs from a Great Horned Owl last night. I'm tired and hungry. Under my black cap, I peer with my red eyes over our nest of sticks in the crook of this ancient Ponderosa Pine. The sunrise casts shadows.

We have survived 20 sunrises but have 10-16 more until our babies peck their way out. Then, another 27-34 until our babies can fledge.

I remember how my mate soared above me during courtship and how quickly his needle-sharp talons could squeeze the life out of a future meal. My tummy rumbles. He knows his job is to feed me while I incubate these eggs. Suddenly, there he is soaring above with a limp robin clutched in his talons. *Cack-cack-cack-cack* I cry. *Welcome home.*

Months later in the nest,

the Cooper's Hawk serves her six offspring a squirrel,

shelters her fledglings,

soon to take flight before the fires begin.

Oh Ponderosa!
by Catalina Marie Cantú

I hug
your bright orange, brown irregular fissures
inhale the distinctive whiff of vanilla or butterscotch tepenes,
chemicals in the bark that act as a natural fungicide/insecticide
and benefit your immune system.

Imagine if we humans had that
on our exterior to protect us.

Named Ponderosa by a botanical explorer
for your "ponderous" size,
your true name in Sahaptin
is spoken by the Yakama people.

I bow
my head with respect
for all you have given
over the centuries
gum as a salve
needles and fine roots for basket making

pitch for glue and waterproofing
seeds and the sugar rich inner bark for food
stems and limbs for building and firewood,
trunks for dugout canoes
and then thousands of trees
to build houses, stores, barns.

I look
up at your crown
as it touches the sky
steady spirals of long limbs,

foliage of two-to-five-inch needles
in groups of three. Large buds at the tip

of branches protected by a tuft of long needles.
Often protecting young trees from fires.

How many fires have you survived?
With taproots eight times your height in length
you connect to water
far below the surface.

In the Cascade Rain Shadow
your resistance to drought and
fire make you the ideal tree.

You, oh gentle giant
are my favorite tree
discovered on
a family road trip

My first Ponderosa
pinecones
rest in a shoe box
cradled in hawk feathers.

Wenas Wildlife Area

The Wenas Wildlife Area, located southwest of Ellensburg and northwest of Selah in Yakima and Kittitas counties, is a diverse and scenic landscape managed by WDFW. Covering over 106,000 acres, the wildlife area includes shrubsteppe, riparian corridors, and higher-elevation forested habitats. Its varied terrain supports a diversity of wildlife, including elk, deer, bighorn sheep, turkey, chukar partridge, quail, and a range of small mammals, upland birds, raptors, and reptiles.

Approximately 75,000 acres of the Wenas Wildlife is shrubsteppe habitat, a diverse and arid ecosystem found in Eastern Washington. Many species, including the greater sage grouse, sagebrush sparrow, burrowing owl, Townsend's ground squirrel, and northern sagebrush lizard can only be found in shrubsteppe. With an estimated 60 to 80% loss or degradation of shrubsteppe habitat statewide, protecting and enhancing this landscape is a primary goal of the Wenas Wildlife Area.

Since fall 2021, the Wenas Wildlife Area has been restoring the 150-acre Bull Pasture site, beginning with a two-year chemical fallow to control invasive species that were persistent throughout the site. In fall 2023, the site was seeded with a native grass mix of shrubsteppe species. On-going weed control efforts will target broadleaf weeds, specifically Russian thistle, as the native grasses establish. In fall 2025, the Rocky Mountain Elk Foundation, which also provided grant funding, will be volunteering with WDFW to seed native forbs to enhance forage diversity.

Similar restoration projects are underway throughout the Wenas Wildlife Area, including the McCabe restoration site, where 60 acres were seeded with native species. Both the McCabe and Bull Pasture restoration sites provide critical winter range for elk and mule deer, and the species are often seen grazing from each site to the top of Umtanum Ridge.

Since 2021, large-scale shrub planting efforts have helped restore wildfire-impacted areas. Approximately 40,000 native shrubs, including big sagebrush, antelope bitterbrush, Woods' rose, golden current, serviceberry, and blue elderberry, have been planted to improve habitat and wildfire resilience across the Wenas Wildlife Area.

The Wenas Wildlife Area offers diverse recreational opportunities, from big game hunting to hiking along trails. The upper Wenas Valley, recognized as an Important Bird Area by the Audubon Society, is a hotspot for birdwatchers, hosting species such as the northern goshawk and white-headed woodpecker.

As recreation pressure grows, WDFW works to balance public access with habitat protection and restoration. Increased recreation activity can impact wildlife, altering behavior, increasing stress, and degrading sensitive ecosystems. To address these challenges, WDFW has developed a 10-year Recreation Strategy aimed at balancing public access with the protection of wildlife and habitats. This strategy emphasizes proactive planning and sustainable management of recreational activities to minimize disturbances to sensitive species and critical habitats.

At the Wenas Wildlife Area, WDFW is implementing this strategy by improving trail planning, installing interpretive signage, and monitoring recreation impacts. Efforts include consolidating trails to reduce habitat fragmentation, installing interpretive signage to educate visitors about sensitive ecosystems like biological soil crusts—delicate communities of cyanobacteria, mosses, and lichens that stabilize soil, retain moisture, and support plant growth—deploying monitoring equipment to better understand patterns of trail and road use in the wildlife area, and collaborating with partners (e.g., AllTrails, Manastash Ridge Trails Committee, Washington Trails Association) to ensure sustainable, responsible use of the trail network. These measures help mitigate disturbances to wildlife, particularly habitat specialists and species with vulnerable reproductive stages, which are more sensitive to human activity.

By focusing on responsible recreation, WDFW aims to ensure that the Wenas Wildlife Area remains a place for both recreation and wildlife habitat. As climate change intensifies stressors like drought, wildlife, and habitat shifts, managing recreation pressures becomes even more critical to maintaining resilient ecosystems that can support both wildlife and people in a changing climate.

Wenas Quartet
by DJ Lee

I. Fog and Memory

We wake in the 1911 Masonic Temple,
its grand second empire façade—Hilton now—
shouldering the first gray light.
Down the highway, by the Yakima River Walk,
the fog unfolds, presses hands to the land.
Steph appears as she was then: small, trusting,
blood and innocence pooling
on gashed knees. She didn't cry—
bone white, asphalt black—
she bore the wound in silence
and I, her mother, was not there.
I was somewhere between Milton and Wordsworth
grasping for the false permanence of meter,
believing education could be my sanctuary,
while the world carved itself into her skin.

What land fashions resilience from rock?
What love lets it bleed?

Rest Haven Road unspools:
a recollection of graduate students crammed
into borrowed cars on I-82,
commuting to the university
past cottonwoods ghosted by winter,
branches black with vultures that weren't vultures—
peahens, though we still called them vultures
because belief lingers longer than fact.

Convoys passed us, desert-brown tanks lumbering
toward the firing center and
soldiers practicing the art of survival,
the geometry of dodging bullets
in a widening gulf of war.

The fog thickens,
every bare branch of the cottonwoods
gestures, saying: *Listen*.
What lies ahead is unknowable.
What lies behind, erased.

II. The Land Speaks

In Selah, in a house rented from a landlord friend,
the arms of a giant maple supported us,
trunk anchoring the backyard in permanence,
canopy stretched wide,
spilling green shadows across our days.
The tree was not just there—it *was* the yard,
roots tangling with the soil of our lives,
a cathedral of leaves where sunlight
filtered down like prayer,
shading us from the press of the world.
Still, news spilled its own shade—
sand from a distant desert swept through our screens,
columns of smoke rose like severed branches,
where oil fires blackened the Earth.
and the skies mirrored lamentation.

Later, during the summer of endings,
we lived beneath the shadow of towers falling,
like the walls of Jericho,
ash drifting like incense
over cities too far to touch.

Selah, stop and listen.

Now, as we drive, strip malls bleed
into a slow topography of cows and goats,
into a barn graffitied with Sasquatch,
into the stubborn thought of rabbitbrush,

sage on sage, white and beige,
until the apple orchards appear in their strange grids,
until hop fields hum with a mean symmetry.
A border collie spirals endlessly,
donkeys flick their ears at the wind's relentless questions.
Steph flourished here,
even as we threaded ourselves through days of hurry—
turgid faculty meetings,
aging parents in Spokane,
flights to factories in Europe and Asia—
and we never once stepped into the Wenas.

What kept us from its open hands?
The pull of elsewhere, the ceaseless grind.
The way duties devour hours.

Sun cracks the fog,
thin light skims a surprise roadside cemetery—
small, quiet, unremarkable.
We stop and remember
how small we were
against this place,
its seasons and silence.

III. Elk and Echoes

The Wenas, carved for wintering elk,
writes itself on the earth:
the weight of hooves tracing paths,
their marks a scripture we try to follow.
We cross Umtanum Creek,
ice shivering underfoot,
the sun a question cresting the ridge.
Four crows pivot above us,
a bald eagle perched in the bare hand of a snag.
Mule deer drift through the sage.
Ahead, seventeen turkeys lurch, their squeaks and gobbles

absurd yet holy—
as if they understand the gravity of the season.

The observatory rises in the distance,
its ashen dome watching the stars.
We think of Mauna Kea,
of telescopes on sacred ground,
and here, too, how the stars are measured above
while below, chukar scatter in the sagebrush,
and the Pshwánapam remember the Wenas
as a corridor of trade and song.

IV. Dusk and Departure

Snowshoers greet us on the road,
laughter sharp in the brittle air.
The road is closed, we say.
You're lucky, an old man replies,
Tank traps are down there.
And I remember the convoys:
khaki bodies armored in steel and war,
dreaming of sandstorms halfway across the world.

Dusk kneels over the hills as we leave,
past Selah, the house where we lived before—
before the towers fell,
before fires scoured the sage,
before we thought of climates, of change.
The giant maple is gone now,
stacked into firewood, its rings unread.

Selah, pause and reflect.

The Wenas bears witness,
its fire scars black on beige,
its grasses dormant.
This land knows wounds—

Steph's knee, split open on asphalt,
her silence bearing the weight of healing,
a mother's love too often late
but learning to kneel beside pain.

The Wenas stands,
not wasteland, not forgotten.
A place of crepuscular light,
of rabbitbrush and buckwheat,
of histories buried but not erased.

The Wenas is witness,
to the landlord's daughter
who took starts from the maple,
nursed them into seedlings,
and planted them in a valley in Indiana,
where they are knee-high now,
roots reaching into new Earth.

The elk move on, their paths
crossing ours, their stories
murmur in the snow
saying, *Wounds close,*
love learns, seeds take root.

Klickitat Wildlife Area

The Soda Springs Unit, part of the Klickitat Wildlife Area, offers a range of recreational opportunities amidst its diverse habitats and landscapes. Located approximately 15 miles west of Goldendale in Klickitat County, this unit spans multiple habitats, including conifer forests, oak woodlands, riparian zones, grasslands, and talus slopes. The unit is also near the Klickitat River, a free-flowing tributary of the Columbia River that originates on the slopes of Mount Adams. Named after a naturally carbonated spring along the river's lower end, the Soda Springs Unit is not only habitat for fish and wildlife but also a destination for those seeking access to Washington's unique ecosystems.

Aerial view of a herd of 49 elk traversing a snowy hillside in the fog within Game Management Unit (GMU) 382, East Klickitat County. Winter conditions drive elk to lower elevations in search of forage, highlighting their seasonal movement patterns in Washington's shrubsteppe landscape. Photo credit: WDFW.

Recreational activities here are as varied as the landscape, with visitors enjoying hunting, fishing, camping, hiking, and wildlife viewing. In spring, wildflower enthusiasts explore the blooming meadows, while horseback riders and cyclists navigate the trails throughout the warmer months. During winter, the unit transforms into a hub for Nordic skiing and snowshoeing, offering Washingtonians year-round access to nature.

Forest management efforts on the Soda Springs Unit are aimed at improving forest health, making it more resistant to wildfires, and protecting important wildlife habitats, particularly for the state-endangered western gray squirrel. The western gray squirrel, which was recently uplisted to endangered status in Washington State, depends on healthy, forested environments to thrive. This species faces serious threats from habitat loss, wildfires, and competition with invasive species. Western gray squirrels play a critical role in forest ecosystems by spreading seeds like acorns and pine nuts, helping forests regenerate and thrive.

In 2018, a forest thinning project was completed on 161 acres to create a healthier, more resilient forest. The thinning reduced tree competition for water and nutrients while lowering the risk of large, destructive wildfires. Surveys were conducted to locate western gray squirrel nests, and a 25-foot buffer was maintained around each nest to avoid disturbances. Brush and branches were cleared to minimize fire risks, and cultural resources were carefully preserved. This project demonstrated that forest management could effectively balance wildfire prevention and wildlife protection.

Building on this success, a second phase of the Forest Health Enhancement Project began in 2023 on the Soda Springs Unit of the Klickitat Wildlife Area, aiming to thin between 247 and 270 acres of western gray squirrel-occupied forest. Surveys in 2023 identified 797 nests within the project area, and adjustments were made to protect these nest trees. By promoting forest health and wildfire resistance, this ongoing work supports the long-term persistence of western gray squirrels in the wildlife area while providing a more open understory to reduce fire spread. This carefully planned approach continues to serve as a model for managing critical wildlife habitats in fire-prone landscapes.

Soda Springs Wildlife Area
by Jim Cantú

Standing in the shadow of majestic Pahto,
Though recent immigrants call it Adams,
I look around for a ticket window.
Certainly, all this beauty must have a fee.

But here, in this rugged splendor, how do you set an entry fee?
What is that scrub oak worth?
It won't yield much lumber.
Is the value only in board feet?

Can we place a value on the feat of wind carried caresses,
Nourishing sunlight kisses and shy moon glow glances?
How nature has carefully sculped these trees and this landscape.
Like a careful craft person with a vision for breathtaking wonder.

Here in an area rarely touched by human hands,
Every creature plays its' part.
Even the endangered western gray squirrel.
How can one so small play such a vital role in this biosystem?

Some say over half the nuts hidden are "forgotten."
They admit that squirrels play a key role in seed distribution for the forest.
Perhaps our small friends are "remembering-to-forget" some of the seeds.
Perhaps they know where new growth is needed.

How do we measure the value of providing our children and
Our children's children, with a glimpse at the miracles that nature crafts?

Four western gray squirrels on Klickitat Wildlife Area. Photo credit: WDFW.

COLUMBIA PLATEAU ECOREGION

Columbia Plateau Ecoregion
Poet Inés Hernandez-Ávila

Swanson Lakes Wildlife Area
Poet Jon K. Culp

Methow Wildlife Area
Poet Subhaga Crystal Bacon

Sunnyside-Snake River Wildlife Area
Poet Linea Jantz

Columbia Plateau Ecoregion

The Columbia Plateau Ecoregion, stretching across much of eastern Washington, is a vast landscape shaped by ancient lava flows and the Missoula floods. Part of the larger sagebrush biome, this semi-arid region experiences cold winters, hot, dry summers; and annual precipitation ranging from 6 to 30 inches. At its heart lies the shrubsteppe, a habitat traditionally referred to as "rangeland." This name, however, undermines its complexity—dominated by towering shrubs that first catch the eye, the true richness of the shrubsteppe lies beneath the canopy in its grasses, wildflowers, lichens, and other small but vital components. It is a "forest" of a different kind, where everything from tall sagebrush to tiny mosses weave together into a complex ecosystem.

The Columbia Plateau's habitats, including grasslands, riparian zones, wetlands, and basalt cliffs, create a mosaic of habitat that sustains a remarkable array of species. Sagebrush obligates like sharp-tailed grouse, sage grouse, and pygmy rabbits depend on this ecosystem for survival, alongside mule deer, pronghorn antelope, yellow-headed blackbirds, raptors, white-tailed jackrabbits, and many more species.

Over the past century, human activities like agriculture, livestock grazing, and the spread of invasive species have transformed the Columbia Plateau, degrading nearly 60 to 80% of its original shrubsteppe habitat. Fertile lands have been converted to croplands, while overgrazed areas are frequently dominated by invasive grasses such as cheatgrass and medusahead. These grasses dry out early, creating dense, flammable fuel beds that ignite easily and spread fire rapidly. Historically, wildfire was a natural and beneficial disturbance in shrubsteppe ecosystems, preventing overgrowth, recycling nutrients, and encouraging native plant regeneration. Low-intensity wildfires maintained a mosaic of habitats that supported diverse wildlife, including sage grouse and other species dependent on open, mixed landscapes. However, invasive grasses have upset this balance, driving hotter, more frequent wildfires that native species cannot withstand.

Restoring natural fire cycles and managing invasive species are essential to preserving the shrubsteppe's ecological health and resilience. Climate change worsens this issue by driving hotter, drier summers, leading to more frequent and severe wildfires. These create disturbances that promote the spread and establishment of invasive grasses, which in turn fuel even more intense fires—reinforcing a destructive feedback loop that threatens the ecosystem's resilience.

The Washington Shrubsteppe Restoration and Resiliency Initiative (WSRRI) emerged in response to the catastrophic 2020 Labor Day wildfires, which burned over 500,000 acres of critical shrubsteppe habitat. This initiative builds on prior restoration efforts to address both the long-standing challenges of habitat degradation from agriculture, overgrazing, and invasive species and the escalating threat of increasingly frequent and severe wildfires. The WSRRI focuses on replanting native grasses, shrubs, and forbs to stabilize soils, reduce erosion, and curb the spread of invasive species like cheatgrass, which fuel a destructive feedback loop of wildfire and habitat loss. Collaboration is a cornerstone of the initiative, with WDFW partnering with federal, state, tribal, and local organizations to implement large-scale habitat restoration projects. These efforts are designed not only to recover areas impacted by wildfires but also to proactively build resilience into the landscape, ensuring that the shrubsteppe ecosystem can better withstand future climate-driven challenges. Through targeted restoration, community engagement, and coordinated action, the WSRRI aims to protect biodiversity, restore ecological balance, and sustain the species and communities that depend on this unique landscape.

The Land that Knows
by Inés Hernandez-Ávila

There needs to be a way that Indian traditions can contribute to the understanding of scientific beliefs at enough specific points so that the Indian traditions will be taken seriously as valid bodies of knowledge.

—Vine Deloria Jr., *Red Earth, White Lies: Native Americans and the Myth of Scientific Fact.* New York, Scribner, 1995.

1.

I write from Patwin land, sending and receiving light from the earth where íinim pike was born, my Niimiipuu mom, where she grew up with her siblings and parents, our sacred family. The Columbia Plateau, the Colville Reservation, where Joseph's band came to live, where our beloved Himatonwayalátkit is buried in the Nespelem cemetery.

I grew up in Galveston, Texas, on an island. My mom's love took me to our other home, her home, often, and she imbued me with her Niimiipuu consciousness without every saying so directly, . . . but still. I am not like some who have walked the land so tenderly all their lives that they know her by heart. I must be truthful. At my age, I am still learning.

But I trust.

I trust our tamalwit, our laws, our teachings that reveal to us how to be Niimiipuu, the real human beings. I trust niimiipuutimtki, to teach us limqístimt, the 'deep language,' the old words, like my Auntie Tillie Red Elk would say, "the big words."

I trust my late Uncle Frank, one of our last fluent speakers, when he told me once, after I asked for advice, "Be bold." kex kuʔús ʔipnim ʔí·ne hihíne ʔú γitpe yóq̇oʔ wé·s ʔí·nimpe timné·pe. The way he told me that first time is in my heart.

I trust myself to write with care.

2.

Climate change. The earth's body, spirit, heart has felt to the core the wars of aggression. The genocide, dispossession, and ethnocide of the original peoples. The ecocide. The twisted way some cultures arrogantly pursue domination, subjugation, objectification, repression, and an un-conscious disconnect with the earth, with wé·tes. Humans and the rest of life become expendable. In the mangled, violent way a society is focused on profit by any means necessary, all of life is reduced to salability, exploitation, and always, the privileging of the few. Capitalism. Rampant. Voracious. Outrageously obscene. The legacy of a society built on lies. A society that dismissed the original peoples and their wisdom. A society that now needs to listen and heed.

What is to be done?

3.

Let's begin with Coyote who, our collective stories tell us, created the Columbia River so that the people could have Salmon. One story says Coyote, battling and finally killing the giant beaver god, created the Columbia River Gorge from the back-and-forth movements of beaver's tail during their struggle.

Another says that a creek became a huge, swirling river, with Coyote being swept over and over by the water. After nearly drowning, he was thrown up onto a bank far away. When he woke up, the buzzards were watching him, trying to decide if he was dead.

"I'm not dead," Coyote told them (and I'm certain he gave them a *look*— you know), and they flew away. He can be quite literal and known for his one-liners.

Make no mistake, Coyote is definitely not dead. And he and the 'Nchi·wana, the Big River, are intimately related, just as he is related to the Snake, Kootenai, Deschutes, Willamette, Pend Oreille, and Yakima, all together the sites of the largest salmon runs on earth.

Coyote, Iceyéye, knows the Columbia and its tributaries are at the heart of the Plateau cultures. He intended it that way. He has been watching. Just as the earth, nuuniim wé·tes has been watching. Just as the ancestors, núuniim titílu have been watching. They are all witness. To everything.

We know about the ancient floods, perhaps the greatest in the world, that left the Columbia's channel scoured down to its basalt layers. Waqíipa. A long time ago. I imagine the force of those waters, charging forth with such power, creating such a tremendously healing installation of nature for the generations to come.

We also know of the dams on the Columbia, and the history of the land at our special water places, from Celilo Falls, Wyam, "echo of falling water," "sound of water on rocks," and Kettle Falls, another of our major ancient fishing sites. Lake Roosevelt flooded Kettle Falls in 1940. We remember the Ceremony of Tears, when the peoples' tears joined the tears of the waters at the inundation of the falls.

Iceyéye says, "Restore the falls."

4.

As Indigenous peoples we do our best to know our lands, deeply, intimately. Our lives and worlds depend on our knowing. For sustenance, for the continuance of our richly intricate cultures. When intruders come onto a land and into a home to steal, or to occupy without permission, it is called theft and squatting. Both are illegal. No word of this in our country's founding documents, other than to call Native peoples "merciless savages." A nation founded on lies cannot withstand the tests of time. Unless, finally, there is an admission. The original peoples of this hemisphere are the ones who know best how to care for this portion of the earth. The ones who have been watching are also waiting.

5.

We want the Land Back.

Recently, a man named Ernie Figlenski, guided by his conscience, and his love for the land, made it possible for his former 9,243 acre ranch to return to the peoples of the Colville Confederated Tribes. By Figlenski's admission, he did so to keep the land in good health and undivided.

The land is back where she belongs, now in excited gentle conversations with the Peoples who know her best. The land is becoming a classroom, an example of what could be more broadly. Sincere gestures of restoration and concern for climate resilience. An acknowledgement of Indigenous wisdom in the stewardship of the earth.

This is a path of choice.

Honoring Prayer for the Twelve Traditional Chiefs
of the Colville Confederated Tribes
by Inés Hernández-Ávila

With deep respect and asking their permission
and the permission of their peoples to name them, I write in honor of

Chief Chiliwist Jim, Methow,
Chief Long Jim, Chelan,
Chief John Harmelt, Wenatchi,
Chief Silicosaskit, Entiat,
Chief Moses, Moses Columbia,
Chief Tonasket, Okanagon,
Chief James Bernard, Lakes,
Chief Kanaqua, Colville,
Chief Jim James, San Poil,
Chief Nespelem George, Nespelem,
Chief Cleveland Kamiakin, Palus, and
Hinmatonwyalátkit/Chief Joseph of the Nez Perce.

Núunim titíluunm wiweʔnekíin ciwéetciwet hiwsíix!

Our ancestors' names are precious.

Walí ·mnekse. I am just thinking.

These titílu, these ancestors, each one, even in spirit, is a leader, an
ʔinoqtiyawáʼt.
They each possess the disciplined wisdom of their teachings,
and himiyuné ·wit, their deep understanding of kinship.

ʔóykalo ·nm hiná ·smicisa ʔoykalo ·na
they all hear us all
ʔoykalo ·
everyone, all the people, including the peoples from the natural world

kuʔús ʔiná ·txiyaksaχ
So I am making a wish.

Núuniim titílu
Luxlukíce, I am worried.
The earth is suffering.

We need your wapá ʸatat, your help.
Your tiwíyekitx, your advice, your counseling

You are the ones who know your languages
and their teachings
You know talapó ·sa, our religion(s)
you know wé ·tes, the earth
kús, the waters
halxpamayá ʸa hí ·semtuks the sun
ciḱetpemeyé ʸe hí ·semtuks the moon
and stars
the sentient intelligence of the lighted earth
our peoples' long memory

You know our medicines and our foods that live in your hearts
You know our rules by which we are to live
the kinship we must share with all living beings
how we must be grateful
to each one of our relatives
to each one of our teachers
saying qe'ciyéwyew to each one

Salmon, nacóʔx̣
deer, ʔímes
bitterroot, łitá ·n
camas, qémes
huckleberry, cemí ·tx
chokecherry,
our first foods
our offerings
our medicines
nuuniim saykáptata

Núuniim titílu
You are in that time that is the all-time
You each have cúukwenin'
the spiritual knowing of our peoples
You each have attained wéeyexnin'
You are true human beings
in spirit now
you see everything
you see the earth's suffering

capaʔlakaʔwiyó ·sa
I am casting light in your direction.
Please
pitamtá ynim
Send me a message.
I hope to receive its ʔilakáʔwit
its brightness
the flame of hope of your response.

I will listen for your songs, your wenípt
in the wind
in the early morning and evening
in the whispers and caresses of my plants
in the rhythms of the rivers
in the taste of our foods
in the familiar smells we know so well
and in my dreams
I long to hear those old-time voices
reminders across time
of our beginnings.

I will receive them in íinim timíne, in my heart
from you, núuniim titílu
and all the ones you represent.

Qe'ciyéw yew for listening
Hetéʔew titílu
Beloved elders.

I Wish I Had My Grandma's Wé·yekin!
by Inés Hernández-Ávila

"I just wish I had my grandma's wé·yekin!"
my mom would say forcefully
when something or someone upset her
A cause for many hmphhhs, and "Oh, for heaven's sakes!"

Her grandma
my great-grandmother
was a tiny woman
Hiyum ʔÁ·tway
Old Grizzly Bear Woman
tiwataʔá·t
feared medicine woman
who worked with Rattlesnake
wé·xpusx̣
was her wé·yekin.

my mom, second oldest of the siblings, would say, "She was just so cute!"
my auntie Dawn, the youngest, would say, "She was scary!"

Hiyú·m Atway
known for her wé·yekin
could make the world tremble
and collapse
but she could also
bring the world back together again
all healed

My mom yearned for her granma's wé·yekin
when something disgusted her
when someone made her so mad
she wanted to whammy them.

I used to laugh and tell her,
"It's a good thing you don't have it!"

But now, as I think of climate devastation,
going back
the sacred places inundated
the rock formations
our ancient literatures
gone
the reduction of fields where the blessed roots are gathered
the rising temperatures
low snowpack
man-made barriers
changes in streamflow
Chinook needing cold streams
Warmer, drier summers causing fire risks
I want to say, for íinim pike,
"I wish I had my great-granma's wé·yekin!"

to help protect our lands
our waters, our animal, plant, and sky relations
to help protect our ways
to help protect our peoples

and to know when to whammy when I must, with all my might.
Yó·qo.

Swanson Lakes Wildlife Area

The Swanson Lakes Wildlife Area, particularly the Swanson Lakes Wildlife Unit, is a critical site for shrubsteppe conservation in Washington. Located within the channeled scablands of the Columbia Plateau, about 10 miles south of Creston in Lincoln County, this area spans 21,000 acres of shrubsteppe and riparian habitats. It provides essential refuge for a variety of species, including mule deer, upland game birds, raptors, songbirds, and a range of reptiles and amphibians. Acquired in the 1990s as part of a Bonneville Power Administration wildlife mitigation project, Swanson Lakes was established with a primary focus on protecting the Columbian sharp-tailed grouse that lives in and depends on Washington's shrubsteppe habitat.

Shrubsteppe habitat in Kittitas County. This landscape, characterized by sagebrush and bunchgrasses, provides important habitat for wildlife and is a critical Washington ecosystem. Photo credit: WDFW.

In September 2020, the Whitney Fire swept through the Swanson Lakes Wildlife Area, leaving a devastating impact. Nearly the entire wildlife area unit burned, destroying native shrubsteppe habitat. This event significantly impacted wildlife, including the sharp-tailed grouse and sage grouse, which rely heavily on the sagebrush-dominated landscape for food and shelter. The loss of sagebrush around an experimental sage grouse lek, already struggling to establish populations, has further complicated recovery efforts for this species.

In the aftermath of the Whitney Fire, WDFW collaborated with the U.S. Bureau of Land Management, the Inland Northwest Wildlife Council, and the Spokane Audubon Society to launch a large-scale restoration effort to rehabilitate the damaged shrubsteppe landscape in the Swanson Lake Unit. Partners secured funding to purchase grass seed and native shrubs and forbs, which were planted across the wildlife unit. Restoration activities included aerially applying seed mixes, using light tillage equipment to prepare the soil, and planting approximately 15,000 shrubs and forbs in the spring and fall of 2021. These efforts aimed to stabilize soils, reduce the spread of invasive species, and restore critical habitats for wildlife.

The restoration efforts at Swanson Lakes Wildlife Area are a localized example of the broader work being carried out under the WSRRI. The initiative's restoration efforts aim to expand existing native, perennial plant communities and reestablish them in areas where they have been lost.

By stabilizing soils, reducing erosion, and controlling invasive species like cheatgrass, the efforts at Swanson Lakes align with WSRRI's mission to build resilience into the shrubsteppe ecosystem. These actions not only support critical species such as the sharp-tailed grouse but also ensure that the broader ecosystem can better withstand the challenges posed by hotter, drier summers that increase the potential for wildfires in the Columbia Plateau. Through collaboration, community engagement, and science-driven action, the work at Swanson Lakes highlights a collective commitment to shrubsteppe recovery and resilience in Washington.

WDFW staff and volunteers from the Inland Northwest Wildlife Council plant native grasses at the Swanson Lakes Unit to replace those burned by the Whitney wildfire. Photo credit: WDFW.

The Rewilding
by Jon K. Culp

Stewardship has history
in these channeled scablands—
where heels touch the soil,
a tension slowly erodes
into a pale blue overhead,
the soil shallow,
the scars run deep.

> *A sharptail grouse prefers*
> *wild rye to winter wheat.*

Cold silver bones of sagebrush
lay scattered like corpses
on a primitive battlefield.
Two plateaus to the south,
survivors huddle together en masse,
staring skyward in their emerald gray.

Rose stems, red and stark against
the buck-tan grass and rye—
a wild wave in her hips. In concert,
dried yarrow in their de-seeded
headdress stand singly and in patches,
silent but the wind whispering among
the low growth, an appeal for healing.

Slender and slumping reeds huddle
a low crescent above the frozen lake—
no ripple or goose on its solid surface,
only a lone distant cloud reflects
silent revolution pushed up from
layered sediment slumbering
beneath the ice. A solitary crack
springs forward toward grassland
on the north shore of the lake.

Coyote and crow tracks imprint
frozen mudded memory until
the sun arcs up from the southern
sky and this land re-generates.

A mule deer enjoys
the company of cows.

Near the south shore, ancient boulders
scatter erratically, some oddly powder-
white in this land of bleak basalt,
others gray-black and fade-rusted
by lichen, some rest near shore,
frozen in place, captured by the lake,
further out some show just a nose,
sniffing at the chill, while others wear
small pock marks as though ancient
birds pecked to crack them for some
volcanic yolk. None lies smooth—
cracked, cratered, carved undulations
introduce familial faces, landscapes
in replica, and extinct animal tracks—
topographical storyboards of a long-ago
journey in the Missoula floods,
migrating from Whitefish to form a fire
ring for a hunting party of the Spokane
Tribe centuries ago, or a fisherman
decades ago, or a range rider
checking on someone else's cows.

A bark of Australian Shepherd
echoes that of the badger.

Shadows of bunch grass
dance in the hazy sun, working
for their warmth. Basalt outcroppings
guard the landscape with rising plateaus,

like harborage risen from the plain
with walls scarred and crumbling,
to protect the native landscape
and creatures from another siege.

From here, the prehistoric mountains
of the reservation to the north watch
with care as ponderosa pines migrate
west encroaching on this ancient
grassland. Prior to privatization,
good fire shepherded roots
and life here. Even that red-tailed
hawk's feathers appear fire-scorched,
though the vole in its talons didn't see it
that way. A playful group of northern
shrike *twit* and *twill* away the quiet,
a decree of coming change.

Minerals and dry grass waft
on a biting wispy wind.
Can you bring back the good fire,
rewild this landscape to thwart
the march of the pines from altering
this land?

The smell of burning
sage brings resiliency,
prosperity, and peace.
Again.

Methow Wildlife Area

The Methow Wildlife Area, spanning over 34,000 acres in Okanogan County, is a cornerstone of conservation and recreation in north-central Washington. Comprised of several units, including the Methow Unit, it provides critical winter range for mule deer and supports a mosaic of habitats from dry coniferous forests to open shrub-steppe and riparian zones. These diverse ecosystems sustain a wide range of species, including elk, black bears, and numerous bird species, while offering visitors opportunities for hiking, fishing, and wildlife viewing.

Historic wildfires have significantly shaped the Methow Wildlife Area, highlighting the importance of fire management and restoration efforts. The Carlton Complex Fire in 2014 and the Okanogan Complex Fire in 2015 burned thousands of acres, leading to large-scale habitat loss and infrastructure damage across the units. In response, initiatives such as the Methow Forest Restoration project aim to reduce overstocked forests to historic densities, mimicking natural fire regimes through prescribed burns and thinning. These efforts not only restore habitat for wildlife but also build resilience against future wildfires, a critical adaptation as climate change intensifies wildfire risks in the region.

Beyond fire management, WDFW also prioritizes protecting wildlife from other growing pressures, particularly human disturbance during critical seasons. To mitigate the growing impacts of human disturbance during the winter recreation season, WDFW has implemented temporary seasonal closures for five units within the wildlife area from December to March. These closures aim to reduce energy stress on mule deer, which can result from increased movement, displacement from forage, and physiological stress triggered by human presence. Mule deer rely on this limited winter habitat to maintain energy reserves critical for survival and reproduction, making these protections essential to sustaining the population.

For these species, winter recreation compounds the mounting effects of climate change and habitat fragmentation, further stressing already vulnerable populations. These closures are part of a broader strategy addressing the cumulative pressures mule deer face, including habitat loss, wildfire, drought, and disease. WDFW's adaptive management efforts include habitat restoration, conservation easements, and strategic land acquisitions. These measures not only support mule deer but also benefit a variety of other species, from predators like cougars and wolves to scavengers such as bald eagles. Public engagement and collaborative planning, including input from the Methow Wildlife Area Advisory Committee and recreationists, ensure that the balance between wildlife conservation and community access is maintained. By prioritizing undisturbed winter habitats, WDFW underscores the importance of sustainable management in the face of increasing recreational pressures and environmental changes.

(above) A pair of mule deer grazing during winter in the Methow. Photo Credit: Alan Bauer.

(at right) A cross-country skier and a dog enjoying groomed trails in the Methow near Pearrygin Lake and the Methow Wildlife Area. Cross-country skiing is a popular winter activity in the Methow Valley, with designated groomed trails providing access to stunning landscapes. While winter closures have been implemented for much of the Methow Wildlife Area from mid-December to mid-April, groomed Nordic ski, fat tire bike, and snowmobile routes remain open for recreation. Photo credit: Emma Follender.

Golden Doe
by Subhaga Crystal Bacon

With the stillness of hills
flanks rise and fall. Tawny
in summer like a fawn,
soon the land will freeze.
Maybe it will burn first,
leave her in patches
of soot and smoke. You see,
it's the landscape I mean,
wildlife area named for
does who live in these grasses.
The does, sight rhyme with *does*
as in those who do, graceful legs,
swiveling ears. Eyes that catch
the light at night like lanterns
bobbing on prows on a dark sea,
their whole bodies move
from their heads. A wildlife
area, named for these mothers
who have their own seasons
to give birth and to die
by arrow, by bullet,
Golden Doe sounds mythic,
captured on a tapestry, an urn,
temporary as the places we name
for them, the land we burn.

N.B. "Golden Doe" and "What Sound Does Our Draining Make" appeared in the
Winter/Spring 2025 Issue of the online journal *Wordpeace* in slightly different forms.

What sound does our draining make?
by Subhaga Crystal Bacon

Today the river runs, yes, still runs, but slim
like the old marathoner who lived on my child-
hood block, who ran and ran, year round
from our town to the sea. Stringy muscles
and an irrepressible urge to move. Run,

even at a lope. These days, the river
is high, though not *as* high, trees
submerged a few feet from shore, rocks
barely visible under spume like pocks on grey
skin. It's June. We used to call it *Junuary*,

burn wood in the mornings to take off the chill.
Now we lift the light-blocking shades and open
the windows at night. Mock orange blossoms
blow like snow. Soil under grass is brown,
no matter how much water we lay down.

There's a drought. Still walking in the trees
where these two liquid bodies meet, the tiny
fall of water on rocks is a thrill.
On dry duff an empty egg, pinhole
where something hungry took the white and yolk,

the embryo of a bird I can't recognize by sight,
even its eponymous shrill, *kill-deer*
I had to look up. Human given name
for what's only a sound, *kill-deer*. Egg,
fragile, sucked empty, like the shell of earth.

Behold the Humble Amphibious Bistort (partial burning haibun): Big
Buck Lake
by Subhaga Crystal Bacon

From US Forest Service *Plant of the Week*

          in wetland habitats   on
          soils, or in   water itself   submerged or floating

     spikes of bright pink   naked   above   oval,
leathery green leaves   on land,   stems   erect
          and   pubescent   leaf blades   sharp-pointed
          underwater   (hairless) stems, leaves,   blunt tipped
blades.

          with spike-like flower clusters.   *Persicaria*   from
the resemblance of   leaves   to those of Peaches

                              Plains   tribes used
as a food source   medicines from the roots, stems,   leaves.
     smartweed   a   sanitized version of   "arsmart" for the
use   in medieval times to relieve itching   of the   posterior.
          in England   smartweeds   in   gold mine
     tailings   accumulate trace amounts of gold into their tissues

                    naked stalk above
               pubescent hairless peaches
                 trace of gold tissues

Balm of Gilead
by Subhaga Crystal Bacon

The dog and I walk in sticky
cottonwood boughs, planted
to recreate the riparian edge,

tributary of the long dammed
Columbia. The trees are young,
red tips like tiny sex organs.

They scent the air like healing salve.
Tires on the highway meld with water
over rocks. Even low, the river hums.

My friend in Olympia said Western
Red Cedars are dying off.
There's not enough moisture in the air,

the Pacific Northwest's moody
grey blanket is motheaten.
There's fog, but it's not enough

to counteract the drought. Death
creeps up the trees, turns
waxy green sprays brown.

It's late October, snow forecast
here in shrub-steppe tomorrow,
early, maybe a sign. No,

it's not enough to save us.
We try to fix what we've broken:
clogged side-channels of the river

cleared, the logs in a new jam
singing in the center where
fish grow on trees.

com   e   back   wildlife

protect mule deer.

n   o

hunting   the deer

protect

mule

deer   .

feed   D   e e   r
in

winter.

Re   Wild
the
D   e   er.

protect   mule deer

.

recreation

create s   angst.

mule deer   decline

mule deer

going

wildfires

kill

burn

coverage   .

Human   s

walking   dog   s

bother   deer

.

people

drought,   wildfire,

disease   Roadkill

habitat

los   s   .

Deer are

green

shoots   are   vulnerable

deer

a　　r　　　　　e

good-

deer

deer

deer

st　　o　　　　　p　　　　　　　hunting

n　　o　　　　　　　　　　hunting

Mule deer are

wild　　　　　　　.

Mule deer are

pr　　　　　eci　　　　　ou

s　　　　　　　　.

deer-

recommend　n　o　　　　hunting

hunting season　　s

push　deer around

pressure　deer

wildlife

                                       wildlife

                   respond

respond

      t   o

                                  the Golden Doe

The Big Buck

—An Erasure Poem by Subhaga Crystal Bacon

N.B. Source: "OK County commissioners back WDFW's wildlife area closures plan," by Marcy Stamper in the Methow Valley News on November 23, 2023. https:// methowvalleynews.com/2023/11/23/ok-county-commissioners-back-wdfws-wild- life-area-closures-plan/

Sunnyside-Snake River Wildlife Area

The Sunnyside Unit, part of the Sunnyside-Snake River Wildlife Area, encompasses 2,741 acres of primarily deeded land along the Yakima River, 1 mile north of Mabton and 5 miles south of Sunnyside. This unit features a mix of agricultural fields interspersed with diverse habitats, with 90% of its area located within the Yakima River floodplain. Spanning 13 miles of riverfront, the unit includes wetland vegetation, riparian woodlands, upland bunchgrass areas, and isolated stands of aspen, cottonwoods, and willows. These varied habitats provide critical ecosystem services and support a wide array of wildlife.

View of habitat on the Sunnyside Wildlife Area Unit. The Sunnyside Unit features a diverse mix of wetland vegetation, riparian woodlands, upland bunchgrass areas, and isolated stands of aspen, cottonwood, and willow, providing essential habitat for a variety of wildlife species. Photo credit: Alan Bauer.

Management of the Sunnyside Unit focuses on conservation and habitat restoration, particularly enhancing wetland and floodplain habitats. Efforts include planting native grasses, controlling invasive species like Russian olive trees, and managing water levels through irrigation systems. These wetlands, fed by irrigation ditches, natural springs, and sub-irrigation from the Yakima River, create vital habitats for waterfowl such as mallards, wood ducks, and cinnamon teal. The area also supports upland birds like California quail and pheasant, migratory species like geese and ducks, and non-game birds such as bald eagles, burrowing owls, and sagebrush sparrows. Additionally, mammals like bats, black-tailed jackrabbits, American badgers, and mule deer thrive in these restored habitats. With opportunities for birdwatching, hunting, and fishing, the Sunnyside Unit serves as both as wildlife habitat and a valued destination for recreation.

The Sunnyside Headquarters Unit also plays a vital role in bat conservation efforts, particularly in monitoring and combating white-nose syndrome (WNS). This deadly fungal disease, caused by *Pseudogymnoascus destructans*, has killed millions of bats across North America since 2006, with mortality rates reaching up to 100% in some colonies during hibernation. Although the disease was first identified in Washington in 2016, its impact on western bat populations is still unclear, as many bats in Washington do not hibernate in large colonies like their eastern counterparts. This difference could influence the disease's spread in the region.

A maternity colony near the Sunnyside Unit serves as a control site for statewide white-nose syndrome monitoring, providing critical data to understand and address the disease's impact on bats in Washington. In 2023, a bat swab from the unit tested positive for the fungus responsible for WNS, underscoring the importance of ongoing monitoring. Recent efforts have included trapping and sampling bats from the maternity colony— groups of pregnant bats that gather in the spring to prepare for giving birth. These initiatives are part of a novel approach exploring the use of naturally occurring bacteria as a potential probiotic treatment to mitigate the effects of WNS. Protecting bats, which play a vital role in ecosystems as insect controllers and pollinators, remains a key conservation goal for WDFW.

In addition to disease, bats are increasingly vulnerable to climate change, which impacts their survival and reproduction. Rising temperatures and declining moisture levels in arid regions can directly affect roost conditions and water availability, especially for females nursing pups in summer. While bats may adapt to changing climates by shifting their ranges, habitat loss, climate change, and WNS collectively pose significant threats to their populations. Monitoring efforts at the Sunnyside Headquarters Unit provide essential data to address these challenges, helping wildlife managers track the spread of WNS and implement strategies to conserve bat species under these growing pressures.

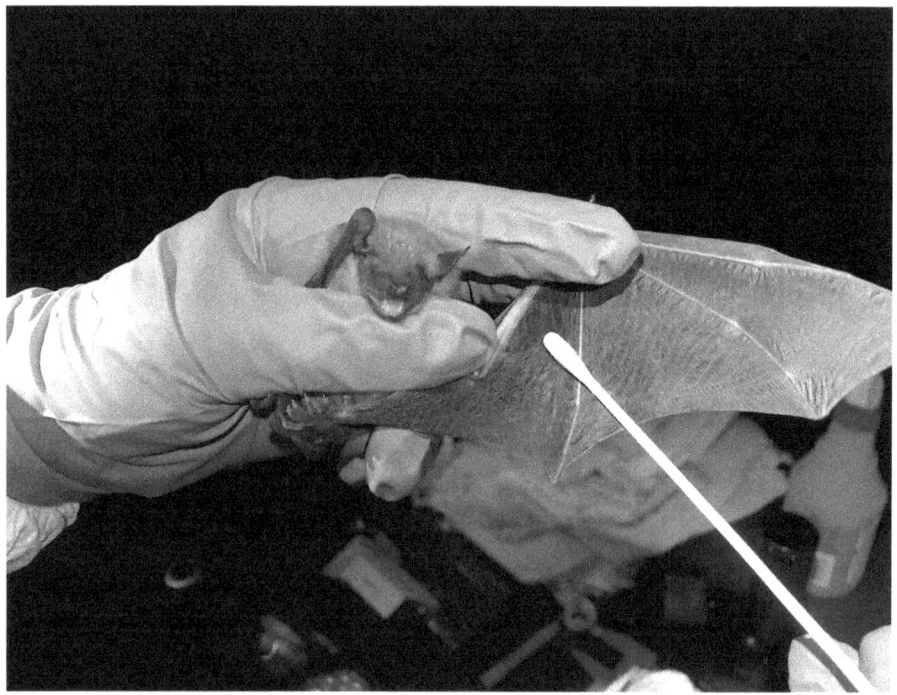

Big brown bat is sampled for white-nose syndrome. Photo credit: WDFW.

Sage Grouse Kyrielle
by Linea Jantz

the snake suns on the prairie's grave
spacious skies darken– a different amber wave
the third dust storm in as many weeks
the sagebrush burns. we only mourn the trees

I crouch, unwilling to leave the snake to die
palm beneath his head, I gently meet his eye
his tongue flickers my way curiously
the sagebrush burns. we only mourn the trees

his scales rasp, wrap the pulse of my wrist
I hear the flames crackle. he seems undistressed
350 species depend on sagebrush for their needs
the sagebrush burns. we only mourn the trees

I carry the snake until the air grows colder
coils settled onto a patch of moondust shoulder
shrugging butterflies into the summer heat
the sagebrush burns. we only mourn the trees

I've never seen a sage grouse in thirty-six years
and for most of that time I've lived near here
there used to be millions. now maybe 200,000 breathe
the sagebrush burns. we only mourn the trees

Land Above the Water
by Linea Jantz

Rattlesnake Mountain is quiet
no rush of traffic in the background
no hikers chatting

only the wind in the grass
the trill of a meadowlark on a nearby fence post

my guide says to stand on this mountain as the sun rises
is to watch light dance across the entire sky
he also says to be careful here when it's windy

we stand in a field of nodding lupine
western stoneseed
death camas

an infusion of stoneseed root in water
drunk once a day is natural birth control

death camas are pollinated by a special type of bee
ground-dwelling, able to survive the pale flower's toxic nectar
one of this sisterhood hums lazy past my knees

the Yakama Nation call this mountain Laliik
land above the water

13,000 years ago this was an island of safety in the Missoula Floods
some people doubt the tribes have been here that long
but they all have the same stories

the Colville
the Nez Perce
the Umatilla
the Wanapum
the Yakama

all agree

Laliik is sacred
there are medicines and foods here that grow nowhere else

during World War II, this land was seized by the U.S. government
a buffer against the nuclear experiments at Hanford

a missile base squatted at the end of this ridge
until we replaced the missiles with a telescope
always an eye on the sky

the year I graduated from college, something different began
the process of returning Laliik to herself

today a herd of elk pour across the opposing hillside
their breath a song made cloud
my curls snap at the wind like irritable dogs

no bees today
the mountain is quiet

A Reckoning in the High Desert
by Linea Jantz

in the high desert near a mountain of snakes
burrowing owls nest in barrels
yellow eyes blink in the dark
wire cages
beaver deceivers
muzzle the mouths of garrulous ditches
we monitor the bats closely
we don't need a Pulp Fiction moment
snorting powdered sugar in the bathroom
a whole colony executed
due to one white nose
a herd of giant elk stream over the hills from Hanford
do they glow in the dark?
they bugle snow geese to the sky
a pulsing feathered mass
at least one species is multiplying
in this changing climate
the frog doesn't notice
he should jump before it's too late
a showgirl headdress of nodding fronds
phragmites nobility of grasses hold court
shorebirds skitter, skate the water's edge
cattails choke the stream
we push them back
the blackbirds' hoarse screams
a field of milkweed whispers in the sun
larval monarchs climb slow
ducks chortle from their boxes
wings flutter in the dark
we count them all

BLUE MOUNTAINS ECOREGION

Blue Mountains Ecoregion
Poet CMarie Fuhrman

W.T. Wooten Wildlife Area
Poet Jeanne Morel

Asotin Creek Wildlife Area
Poet Amelia Díaz Ettinger

Blue Mountains Ecoregion

The Blue Mountains Ecoregion, located in the southeastern corner of Washington and extending into Idaho and Oregon, is a rugged landscape characterized by deep river canyons, high plateaus, and expansive coniferous forests. Formed by uplifting Columbia River basalt flows and sculpted by the Snake and Grande Ronde Rivers, this region features topography with elevations ranging from 750 feet along the Snake River to 6,387 feet at Mount Misery. The area encompasses some of Washington's most intact habitats, with diverse vegetation shaped by its varied elevations and precipitation levels, which range from under 10 inches in canyon areas to over 50 inches in the wilderness.

Dominated by Douglas fir and ponderosa pine at lower elevations and transitioning to subalpine fir and Engelmann spruce in higher elevations, the Blue Mountains also support native grasslands, shrublands, and dense canyon vegetation. Springs and alpine lakes dot the landscape, further enhancing its ecological complexity. This ecoregion is important habitat for hundreds of wildlife species, including Rocky Mountain elk, black bears, golden eagles, and cavity-nesting birds such as woodpeckers and bluebirds. Anadromous fish like Chinook salmon and steelhead rely on its streams and rivers throughout the region, though many populations have been diminished and are now listed as threatened or endangered. With much of the land managed by federal and state agencies, including the Umatilla National Forest and WDFW's Asotin and Chief Joseph Wildlife Areas, the Blue Mountains remain a vital ecological and recreational resource increasingly impacted by habitat loss, rural development, and climate change pressures.

The Blue Mountains face multiple climate-driven challenges that impact both forests and aquatic ecosystems. Rising temperatures, declining snowpack, and shifting precipitation patterns are altering the hydrology of the region. Lower elevations are projected to experience longer, drier summers, increasing moisture stress on vegetation and contributing to higher wildfire risk. In contrast, warmer winters will lead to more precipitation falling as rain rather than snow, reducing snowpack and affecting water availability in the dry season. These shifts threaten both aquatic habitats—increasing winter flood risks and reducing summer flows critical for fish survival—and forest health, exacerbating drought stress, tree mortality, and insect outbreaks.

Wildfires are expected to become larger and more intense, driven by a combination of warming temperatures, increased fuel loads from past fire suppression, and drier summer conditions. Fire-dependent species, such as ponderosa pine, may continue to persist, while forests dominated by fire-intolerant species could face significant restructuring. The spread of invasive grasses, such as cheatgrass and ventenata, is another major concern, as these species thrive in post-disturbance environments and alter fire cycles by increasing fine fuels.

Efforts to reduce forest density, restore fire-adapted landscapes, and manage invasive species will also play a key role in increasing ecosystem resilience to the impacts of climate change. By addressing these challenges, the Blue Mountains can continue to provide critical habitat for wildlife, support sustainable recreation, and maintain the ecological functions that define this unique ecoregion.

Antelope Bitterbrush
by CMarie Fuhrman

Feathers from the breasts
of Finch, Meadowlark, and Western Tanager
have been buried by ancestors

They rise as bitterbrush. Melodious
yellow blooms chirping
from the thin boned branches—
and the buttery smell undoes even the rain.

Walking Camp Creek in June
by CMarie Fuhrman

I've come alone. The dogs can't climb over the trees
that have fallen across the narrow path once a road.

The creek has gone down and yet the high water mark
leaves brown soil black. This is where I find arrowheads

and trash. But tonight I'm not looking. The dream
of my life is to walk along companionable streams

to their source. I have done this now. More than once.
Finding the place in the granite where water wept silver.

And I have placed my lips against the rough and lichen
and known nothing more pure. But nature has her guards,

Too. And tonight, they are out en masse. They see me.
They smell me before I am anywhere that granite breast.

And, proboscis unsheathed, they win. I climb from the creek
bed to the shoulder of the drainage. Sometimes its like that.

What you think you need from that deep creek, that water,
is not what you need at all. Sometimes nature guides you

In mysterious ways. Me, I reached the ridgeline in time

To see a mother elk as she cleaned the vernix from her calf.
And her calf, yet unbothered by whatever guards the source,

took her first certain steps toward eternity.

Lesson
by CMarie Fuhrman

It's July and you are in an alpine meadow.
It is bright with buttercup.
Hardly believable, you ask
Is this heaven?
There is a tree in the meadow. It is as tall
as sunrise, you think that maybe it has lifted
the sun for years with those thick arms, you think
this tree may have birthed sun for you watched it cradle
sun in its arms. So you spread a blanket
on the ground beneath the pine.
And you weave your fingers behind your head—
And you watch as drops of light fall onto your body—
And you listen to the Kinglet that sings from the branches—
And you answer your question
without any help.
With all the help you ever needed.

W.T. Wooten Wildlife Area

The W.T. Wooten Wildlife Area spans over 16,000 acres in southeastern Washington. Established in the 1940s to provide winter range for big game and reduce wildlife-livestock conflicts, the area encompasses a wide variety of habitats. The Tucannon River provides critical habitat for salmonids and other aquatic species, while upland forests of ponderosa pine and Douglas fir support large mammals and birds of prey. Grasslands, shrubsteppe areas, and seasonal wetlands enhance biodiversity, offering vital resources for elk, mule deer, waterfowl, and ground-nesting birds. The Wildlife Area also includes eight artificial lakes and the Tucannon Fish Hatchery, established in the 1950s, which support fishing opportunities and populations of rainbow trout, salmon, and steelhead. These varied habitats attract visitors year-round for activities such as camping, hiking, hunting, fishing, and wildlife viewing.

View of the Tucannon Valley from the W.T Wooten Wildlife Area. Photo credit: WDFW.

The W.T. Wooten Wildlife Area stretches 17 miles along the headwaters of the Tucannon River, a critical habitat for the threatened Lower Snake River spring Chinook salmon. Since 2013, restoration projects funded by the Bonneville Power Administration have focused on improving the river's natural processes and improving salmon habitat.

Key efforts include reconnecting the river to its floodplain by removing or modifying levees, culverts, and other barriers. This allows the river to flow more naturally, restoring side channels, oxbows, and wetlands that provide essential rearing and spawning areas for salmon. Invasive plant removal is an ongoing effort, with native vegetation planted to stabilize streambanks, provide shade, and regulate water temperatures. Large wood structures are being added to the river using helicopters and other tools to create pools and slow water flow, offering shelter and better conditions for salmon at different life stages.

These restoration actions have significantly improved the river's habitat. The floodplain now supports more diverse habitats, reduces sediment loads, and helps stabilize water temperatures, while the added wood structures enhance the structural complexity of the river channel. By restoring natural processes, these efforts provide long-term benefits for Chinook salmon and support the resilience of the Tucannon River ecosystem.

The basins in the Blue Mountain Ecoregion, including the Tucannon River, are predominantly mixed rain-and-snow systems, making them especially vulnerable to the impacts of warming temperatures. Climate projections indicate significant changes in streamflow patterns, with increased winter streamflow resulting from more precipitation falling as rain rather than snow and reduced snowpack. This shift raises the risk of winter flooding and landslides. Conversely, summer streamflow is projected to decline due to diminished snowpack, reduced summer rainfall, and increased evaporation. These changes will likely result in lower summer flows, further stressing aquatic ecosystems during critical periods for fish and wildlife. Additionally, stream temperatures are expected to rise due to warming air temperatures and reduced contributions from snowpack and glaciers. These warmer conditions threaten cold-water species like bull trout and Chinook salmon, which depend on cool, oxygen-rich water for survival during spawning and rearing.

These climate-driven changes underscore the importance of the Tucannon River restoration efforts, which enhance floodplain connectivity, stabilize water temperatures, and provide critical refuge habitats for aquatic species. By addressing these challenges, these projects build resilience into the ecosystem, helping to safeguard the river's aquatic biodiversity amid a rapidly changing climate.

Poet's Introduction for Wooton by Jeanne Morel:

Although I went to college in Walla Walla, a little over an hour drive from the Wooten Wildlife Area, I had never visited it before joining the Writing the Land project. In November 2023 I drove out to the edge with my husband, but we didn't have time to venture further. We returned in the summer and I returned once more in October with a friend who's a research scientist. The area is beautiful—brown hills, a rushing river through the canyon. I left with a feeling of precariousness as I sensed the many layered encroachments of humans on the land. The poem "Brittle Intrusions" was first envisioned as words spaced across the page in precarious balance. As I drafted it, the shape of the poems seemed to emulate the map of the canyon, and I played with that notion a bit. Poems are landscapes in themselves—words situated on an otherwise blank page. Just as there is no one way to read a geographic landscape, there is no one way to read a poem. I hope these poems invite you into their landscapes and the landscapes of the Wooten Wildlife Area.

Out Past Dayton—on a Wildlife Refuge Named for Sheriff W.T. Wooten
by Jeanne Morel

1.

Out the car door blue & then a wild rose
        round hills brown like California

gum weed you said
we walked the wooden bridge across the Tucannon River

bull rush   up the hill Doug Fir
Discover Pass required   Burning of Garbage

Prohibited   so many signs

a splash of red

        some species may be at the limit of their range

2.

mesic habitat
                the ground wet
                [but]   not as much water
                penetrating the soil

for the short term [perhaps 100 years] perhaps
less Douglas Fir   more Ponderosa Pines

3.

litter, illegal drones
dirt bikes tearing up campgrounds
illegal campfires

common sense endangered species
quasi extinction

4.

talk of controlled burns
School Fire 2005   over 51,000 acres

today / these days   firefighters busy
Wooten   low priority   no homes

5.

three federally endangered species

            bull trout
            Chinook salmon
                  steelhead

loss of floodplain connectivity
            increased water temperatures on the Tucannon
                  river restoration projects

contiguity continuity conflict
            out the side window   political banners
span the parking lot

6.

I ask about weeds   those place-based yet dis/placed
unfortunates
displacing others

            you look for yellow starthistle   & another
            we find also   _____

dusted maps   fuzzed borders
wild and artificial

7.

Lakes constructed so many years ago.

A Shifting Glossary of Words on Wooten
by Jeanne Morel

acquisition

>
> (noun) a form of the verb acquire
> 1. an asset or object bought or obtained,
>   typically by a library or museum
>
> etymology: late 14c., "act of obtaining,"
> from Old French *acquisicion* "purchase, acquirement"
>
> Wooten Wildlife Area Acquisition (1941 - 1943)
>
> Purpose—
> 1. to reduce conflicts
>   [between wildlife & farm animals]
> 2. to protect land
>   [both wildlife habitats & outdoor recreation
>   areas]

artificial

> The artificial is always innocent.
>   — Frank O'Hara
>
> So pretty—eight lakes created in the 1950s.

boundary

> (noun) that which indicates the limits of
> anything—a *bound* being the limit or furthest point of
> extension of any one thing.
>
> See: Map [the edge of the known & unknown]
>
> Notice to fisherman
> / Check your fishing pamphlet

climate

> Climate change poses challenges
>   to species & habitats that
>   do not recognize

jurisdictional
natural resource
        boundaries.

conflict

        Wooten Wildlife Management Plan
        Conflict Specialist:

        Document wolves living on
        wildlife areas
        where cattle   grazing

        is permitted. Document
        all wolf/cattle conflicts
        on wildlife areas.

        Climate change consideration:

        Consider how change
        in snowpack and winter
        conditions
        will affect impact
        of conflict.

        See: Values

equilibrium

        [lakes created to improve fishing, stocked w/ hatchery
        reared steelhead or rainbow trout]

fishing

        Perhaps I should not have been a fisherman, he thought.
        But that was the thing that I was born for.

                        —Ernest Hemingway, *The Old Man and The Sea*

map

Imaginary lines intended to mediate
perception
& render the world   rendered.

precarious

(adjective) Rhymes with variance.

values

Neither good poetry nor good science
corroborates
the assumption of
presumed values.

—Forrest Gander

weed

(plural, weeds)

Typically not valued for use or beauty.

Origin

Old English *wēod* (noun), *wēodian* (verb), of
unknown origin;
related to Dutch *wieden* (verb).

Could climate change doom
(diminish?) invasive species? Perhaps
native plant replacements can
be planted—perhaps before
other unwarranted
species get established. Perhaps
there's no need
to weed out the weeds—

The Tucannon River flowing through the W.T. Wooten unit. Photo credit: Alan Bauer.

Brittle Intrusion
by Jeanne Morel

At the picnic table at the   campsite above the canyon   road

        insect   chirp   river   wind   flies   quiet

the calculation of use   combination of fragility

        comes into account

a counting an account   I look at the bugs underneath

        earlier I heard you say   —warmer, longer, dry period

                reckoning intrusion fragility mix of uses

rain/fall   falls less falls less in   lessens

        fall & winter

                an accounting of

more rain more   now will fall   in spring

                playground of the Tri-Cities

        when it's hot here   it's 1000 degrees in

                        the Tri-Cities

the smell of rubber burning on Hartsock Grade

the map shows   sections   calculates   uses mix

                    fragile intrusion reckon

                wreck   wreckage   reckoning

we show up Mondays and clean up the mess

                    this side of the road   Fish & Wildlife

                that side   National Forest Service

enter

interstice   that slim space

Tucannon Campground   ponds stocked   excellent trout

                                                        fishing
insert

                understory   scrub   thicket   forest floor

grip the pencil   stub

                sit unable to grasp   just visiting   still

Asotin Creek Wildlife Area

The Asotin Creek Wildlife Area, part of the Blue Mountains Wildlife Area Complex, spans approximately 36,000 acres of southeastern Washington's rugged terrain. Its steep canyons, rolling uplands, and riparian corridors along Asotin Creek provide critical wintering habitat for elk, mule deer, and other wildlife, including bighorn sheep and black bears. The creek itself is vital for aquatic species, offering essential spawning and rearing grounds for steelhead and Chinook salmon, both of which are listed under the Endangered Species Act. Balancing public recreation such as hunting, hiking, and wildlife viewing with habitat conservation remains a central management priority for the Wildlife Area.

A vista looking north over the North Fork Asotin Creek canyon from the broad open plateau on Smoothing Iron Ridge in the Asotin Creek Wildlife Area. Photo credit: WDFW.

Climate change and historical land use have introduced significant challenges to the area. Warming temperatures and shifting precipitation patterns exacerbate wildfire risks, threaten water availability, and stress native plant communities. The 2021 Lick Creek Fire, which burned tens of thousands of acres in Asotin and Garfield counties, further highlighted these vulnerabilities by damaging riparian zones and upland habitats, leaving soils exposed to erosion and streams vulnerable to sedimentation.

Volunteer work has been an essential part of restoring Asotin Creek Wildlife Area, particularly after the 2021 Lick Creek Fire. After fires burned, volunteers from Rocky Mountain Elk Foundation (RMEF) reconstructed water guzzlers which collect and store water for wildlife such as elk, mule deer, and bighorn sheep. In partnership with WDFW, the RMEF has also helped remove hazardous fencing and re-seed habitat to help keep larger native prairie habitats healthy. These local actions are vital for supporting wildlife in a changing environment and illustrates the impact local Washingtonians can make in the wake of ecological disruptions.

The Macfarlane's Four-O-Clock
Mirabilis macfarlanei
by Amelia Díaz Ettinger

"If, for example, you come at four o'clock..."
             —from *The Little Prince,* by Antoine de Saint-Exupéry

I shall be waiting in a futile attempt to feast
my eyes on your magenta petals trampled
almost to obscurity from years of cattle grazing
and the asphyxiation of cheatgrass

I shall think of you as the colorful dame
of a western saloon, dress in the brightness
of your musk that attracts hawkmoth,
Bombus and bees in these dry canyonlands

Have you known that four o'clock
is also known as the 'witching hour'
in this time of fury and threatened portent
extinction of marvels just like you

but if you stay and prosper along these basalt
rims deep in within these Blue Mountains,
then I will also say, "... then by three o'clock
I shall begin to be happy."

Forests seem to burn constantly now,
by Amelia Díaz Ettinger

and though I have prayed for water all
summer, supplicating the sky
to extinguish this asthmatic smoke,
today, I lower my head as if trapped
under a gray cloud ceiling

this rain announces its reunion
to the ground with her early scent of petrichor
an aroma that should be hope,
but I wish the clouds would leave
selfishly, I want to see an open sky
without the yellow haze

the waters finally arrive, and the dust
like soil trembles with relief as the thick
beads reach the ground's parched skin
the dirt jumps, each drop forms a circle
the dust leaps to join, they make a crown
this is soil and water private celebration.

N.B. This poem previously published: Díaz Ettinger, Amelia. "Forest seem to burn constantly now," Themed Water, Tiny Seed Literary Journal, January 4, 2025.

Pygmy Rabbit
Brachylagus idahoensis
by Amelia Díaz Ettinger

in this sagebrush land, so loved
by big game hunters
of elk, bighorn, and mule deer,

whose heads adorn the open brush
taverns and homes, animals easily seen
atop these lava flows

ridges of dry brush that used to move
to the quiet sound of the pygmy rabbit
—those tiny beings that claimed these hills

the smallest of her kind,
Leporidae, industrious,
she makes her own den,

but her delicate bones are savory
for too many predators, her own blood
a traitor of disease, add these constant fires

that eat at her—
without these soft creatures
the sagebrush no longer moves

no longer sings

NORTHERN ROCKIES ECOREGION

Northern Rockies Ecoregion
Poet Sky M. Pagaling

~

Swanson Lakes Wildlife Area
Poet Linda Russo

Northern Rockies Ecoregion

The Northern Rockies Ecoregion encompasses the rugged landscapes of northeastern Washington. This ecoregion is a refuge for diverse wildlife and home to some of the most intact wildlands south of Canada. Dominated by the Selkirk Mountains and the north-flowing Pend Oreille River, the region features dramatic topography shaped by glacial activity, including U-shaped valleys and high alpine peaks. Elevations range from 1,300 feet along the Columbia River to over 7,000 feet in the Salmo-Priest Wilderness, creating a vertical gradient that supports a diverse array of habitats and species. Influenced by both maritime and boreal climate patterns, precipitation varies widely, from less than 18 inches in southern valleys to over 80 inches in the high-elevation forests of the Salmo-Priest Wilderness, with significant snowpack developing at higher elevations.

Vegetation in the Northern Rockies follows clear elevational zones. Low-elevation forests are dominated by Douglas fir and ponderosa pine, transitioning to grand fir, western hemlock, and western redcedar in mid-montane areas. Higher elevations support subalpine fir, Engelmann spruce, and alpine parklands interspersed with meadows. These ecosystems provide habitat for a variety of wildlife including gray wolves, wolverines, moose and Rocky Mountain elk.

Climate change is intensifying stressors on both forest and aquatic ecosystems in the Northern Rockies. Rising temperatures and shifting precipitation patterns are altering hydrology, with reduced snowpack leading to earlier peak streamflows and lower summer water availability. This disrupts freshwater ecosystems, increases drought stress on vegetation and wildlife, and heightens wildfire risk. Warmer, drier summers are expected to drive more frequent and severe wildfires, particularly in areas where past fire suppression has led to unnaturally dense forests. While fire is a natural and beneficial disturbance to ecosystem health, high-severity wildfires threaten long-term forest resilience.

Warming temperatures and more frequent droughts are increasing tree vulnerability to insect outbreaks across the Northern Rockies Ecoregion. Pine bark beetles have been associated with lodgepole and ponderosa pine mortality in Okanogan and Ferry counties, where stressed trees are particularly susceptible to infestation. Fir engraver beetles have been observed causing grand fir mortality, particularly in drought-weakened stands. In Douglas fir forests of east Okanogan, Ferry, and Stevens counties, secondary bark beetles often exploit damage from Douglas fir engraver beetles, particularly in drought-stressed trees. These opportunistic beetles are more likely to succeed during dry periods, further increasing tree mortality. As climate change intensifies drought conditions, these insect outbreaks are expected to become more frequent, leading to increased tree mortality, shifts in forest composition, and reduced ecosystem resilience across the ecoregion.

Despite these threats, significant portions of the ecoregion remain protected by federal and state agencies, providing vital refuges for species and opportunities for conservation-focused land management. Balancing these efforts with sustainable recreation and resource use is critical to preserving the ecological integrity of this unique ecoregion.

A moose navgates through deep snow in northeast Washington during a WDFW collaring project in February 2025. Photo credit: WDFW.

Aerial view of Sherman Creek Wildlife Area in Ferry County, within Washington's Northern Rockies Ecoregion. The Northern Rockies Ecoregion supports a variety of wildlife and provides critical habitat for species adapted to its rugged terrain and climate. Photo credit: WDFW.

Pend Oreille
by Sky M. Pagaling

I never knew that
Name
The Docks, The Caves
Connected lost boys

The Dam and The Old Dike
Keep foreboding secrets
The alure of mischief

Your current
Pushed, resisted and crushed
Clichés
Perpetual strength

Demanding respect
From adolescent boys
Diving from
Forgotten totems

Perch and Sunfish
Peck at forgotten lines
Bass & Pike struggle
For the right to rule

Your channels
Legends under docks
Legends of those who
Refused to leave

Despite knowing you
My short life
I sometimes forget
Forget you have lived

Lives beyond my sight

My story of you
Is that of excitement
And love

But there are those
Who have walked
Your sandbars
And as they vanished
So did their footprints
Those whose lifetimes
Spent with you
Spent long before
I sat at your shore

I come to you
In need of
Solace
A crying boy

Who misses his father

When society failed
And we were left
Among our thoughts
We ran to you

To remember how we felt
When the beads formed patterns
We recognized

Layers
by Sky M. Pagaling

Nestled in the hides
Of the past
He awakens
To find the warmth of family
Layering skins
Gifts given and respect earned
Emerging into the light
The sun is always
Brighter when the ground
Is frozen

The cold silence
echoes of spirits
dancing atop the snow
the hide beneath my feet
crunches ice crystals
releasing the
anxiety, complacency, regret, anger, sorrow, and truth

I shed my layers, prayers, and defenses
I leap with stinging feet into the cleansing cold
Shock, and then acceptance

I burst through the surface with a gasp
My pores release their heated breath
And my hardship sluffs off

I step from your womb
Anew, reinvigorated
Prepared to do what I must
For my people

Untold
by Sky M. Pagaling

As a child I was told of a people who brought in the company of the
northwest circa 1809.

What of the day
The people first
Came to know
Your kindness

The cool of your touch
The Sustenance of your love
The healing power
Of your songs

Your guidance through birth
Your strength in death
Your unwavering flow
Shaping our world

What of the day
The people first
Ventured to cross
To other banks

Did their paddles
Caress your surface
As your current
Carried them

Did you warn them
Of your depths
Swirl them in your current
Harbor them in your sloughs

What of the day
The people first

Learned of your
Strength

Did their tears
Burn as you
Burdened
Their loss
Lost and wandering, the songs call the people back to their lands and
waters. Their ancestors' voices recorded in the ripples of the current. The
heart of the drum still beats but it's the people who must sing.

Swanson Lakes Wildlife Area – Waikiki Springs Unit

Swanson Lakes and Revere Wildlife Areas, which include the Reardan Audubon Lake Wildlife Area Unit, encompass roughly 25,000 acres of shrubsteppe, grasslands, and wetland habitat in eastern Washington. These areas support mule deer, reptiles and more than 200 bird species including Columbian sharp-tailed and greater sage grouse, which are listed by the state as threatened species.

The Waikiki Springs Unit of the Swanson Lakes Wildlife Area is a 115-acre natural refuge along the Little Spokane River in northeast Spokane, alongside densely populated neighborhoods. This property is named for the numerous springs that flow from the hillside into the river, providing a consistent water supply and stable water temperatures year-round. These springs are part of a unique type of ecosystem entirely dependent on groundwater, known for supporting diverse plant and animal species. Groundwater-fed ecosystems like these are especially resilient to climate stressors, offering a reliable refuge for biodiversity by maintaining water flow during droughts and buffering against extreme heat and warming stream temperatures. The consistent, year-round discharge of cool water helps stabilize aquatic habitats, reducing seasonal fluctuations that can stress species dependent on stable conditions. This hydrology not only supports diverse plant and animal communities but also enhances ecosystem resilience by mitigating the impacts of prolonged dry periods and heatwaves. Waikiki Springs is also an important recreational area for the local community. Visitors to Waikiki Springs can hike, cross-country ski, and snowshoe on miles of trails, and access the river for kayaking and fishing.

Historically, the Little Spokane River supported coho and Chinook salmon populations, central to the health and culture of the Spokane Tribe. Prior to the construction of hydroelectric dams on the Columbia River, Chinook and coho salmon returned annually to spawning grounds in the Spokane River. However, this migration was disrupted when hydroelectric dams were constructed, blocking salmon from their historic habitats. By 1941, the Grand Coulee Dam prevented salmon from reaching nearly half the Columbia River system, including the Little Spokane. These changes have added challenges to salmon recovery efforts in the region.

In 2021, a collaborative effort involving the Spokane Tribe, WDFW, and local non-profits was a turning point in restoring salmon to the Little Spokane River. Fifty adult Chinook salmon were released, a critical first step toward rebuilding this once-thriving population. Projects like this aim to honor the legacy of the Spokane Tribe while enhancing the ecological health and climate resilience of the Little Spokane River for future generations.

View of Waikiki Springs Unit grasses and shrubs in the foreground and the Little Spokane River and forested hill in the background. Photo credit: WDFW.

Impermanent Co-Inhabitance
by Linda Russo

FOREST CARE

walking the gravel path down to the plain

keeping an eye on this mixed conifer-deciduous forest

Nick doesn't like cutting down trees but   *a variety of*
trees in size

sometimes it's got to be done   *a healthy forest*
comprise

a healthy tree won't fall
prey to pine borers   *less competition*
a felled tree won't host   *for water required*
larval-beetle life cycle   *to survive*
the hotter drier

sometimes they've got to be   *climate*
felled to avoid   *that will come*
fatal infestations

TREE

enormous aged   seeds sprouting
cottonwood   on crumbling
supine alive   heartwood flanks
decaying into   cycling again
nooks for   into soil
nestlings   persons

POET

on the new kiosk
Boy Scouts made
someone graffitied *Read*
and *dead poet*

but any poet
is only as dead
as a tree that falls
& is let
to live out
their story

LAND USE

you may walk out to a spring   led by the sound of water

here where the dairy farmer settled and built up house and barn

this is where Nick, upon request, mowed a trail out to the pond

and in this spot one must keep certain weeds in check
                                            (invasive in this place   they know no bounds)

dispersed recreation gives rise to *social paths* & beyond them a fort kids built
that Nick disassembled   & beyond that another fort they will build

                    pick up your trash please   lower your carbon footprint

human presence is permanent for now time brings improvements
            (one man gave a bench to say *thanks for all mothers, especially mine*)

this is where Mary, an everyday walker, watched a turtle lay her eggs
and bury them   here along the path she'd like to name *Turtle Curve*

he near the river where Chinook Salmon may spawn

WILDLIFE SIGHTINGS

moose   elk   bald eagle   cougar   deer   racoon

MORE WILDLIFE SIGHTINGS YET TO COME

SPRINGS*

earth cold waters
gush down the hillside
keep the river
perfectly chilled
for salmon and trout
perfectly cool for prohibited
hot summer swims

springs keep river lives
entangled here in the work
toward restoring
wholeness

---

* in Hawaiian, *wai* means *fresh waters* and *kīkī, to spout*

Poets' and Prose-Writers' Biographies

Julian Ankney is Niimíipuu 'Nez Perce' who works for social justice for Missing and Murdered Indigenous People, as her brother went missing in 2018; Indigenous language reclamation as resistance; and sovereignty and human rights for Indigenous people. She directs Native American Programs at Washington State University. Her work is in *Talking River, Yellow Medicine Review,* and *EcoArts on the Palouse;* on the radio; in the Hearst Museum: *Cloth that Stretches* (2020); and in Fishtrap's *Renewal: A conversation with luk'upsíimey / NorthStar Collective* (2022).

Subhaga Crystal Bacon (they/them), is the author of four collections of poetry including the Lambda Literary Award finalist, *Transitory* (BOA Editions, Ltd., 2023); and *Surrender of Water in Hidden Places*, winner of the Red Flag Poetry Chapbook Prize, 2023; A Pushcart and Best of the Net nominee, Subhaga is a teaching artist working in schools and libraries with youth and adults, as well as private students.

Simmons Buntin is the author of two books of poetry, *Bloom* and *Riverfall*, as well as a collection of community case studies, *Unsprawl: Remixing Spaces as Places*, and *Satellite: Essays on Fatherhood and Home, Near and Far* (Trinity University Press, 2025). He is the founding editor of *Terrain.org* and lives in Tucson, Arizona.

Kathleen Byrd is a writing teacher who resides in Olympia, Washington, within the territory and lands of the Coast Salish People. Her book of poems, *Last Resort,* was published by Last Word Press (2024). She is the fourth poet laureate of Olympia, Washington, where she engages the community with the literary arts connecting to themes of climate change and place. She received an MFA from Western Washington University in 2021.

Catalina Marie Cantú is an Indigenous Mexican/Madeiran multi-genre writer, arts instigator, Jack Straw Fellow and VONA Alum. Her poetry and prose appeared in *La Bloga; Poetry on Buses; Seattle Poetic Grid;* and were anthologized in *Raven Chronicles Take a Stand, Art Against Hate; Writing the Land: Foodways and Social Justice; Indomitable/Indomables A Multigenre Chicanx/ Latinx Women's; The Inspired Poet;* and elsewhere. Cantú is President/Co-founder of La Sala, a Latinx Artists' Community.

Jim Cantú is a Chican@ writer and radio producer who pens poems, prose and personal essays. His work appears in *Writing The Land: Wanderings II, Writing the*

Land: Windblown II, In Xóchitl in Cuícatl : Floricanto: Cien años de poesía chicanx/latinx (1920-2020), Raven Chronicles, the *Seattle Poetic Grid*, and elsewhere. Jim is a graduate of the Artist Trust Literary Edge program and a Jack Straw Writer Program Fellow. He produces Latin@ music and public affairs programs for community radio and volunteers with Latin@ Artist Collective - La Sala Northwest.

Jon K. Culp began writing in the high mountain desert of North Central Washington. His work appears in the *Manastash, Arcturus, Backstory*, and *Percival Review* literary journals, and the digital art series *Stunning Poetry* at Silent Spark Press. He draws from 40 plus years of working in and around natural resources, from wildland firefighting and trail crew boss to water conservationist and even volunteer luge guide at the local course. His writing is an eclectic mix of perceptions of the natural and social world.

Amelia Díaz Ettinger is a Latinx BIPOC poet and writer. Her books include *Learning to Love a Western Sky, Speaking at a Time /Hablando a la Vez, These, These Hollow Bones*, and two chapbooks *Fossils in a Red Flag* and *Self Dissection*. Amelia's poetry and short stories have been published in anthologies, literary magazines, and periodicals. She has an MS in Biology and an MFA in creative writing. Her literary work is a marriage between science and her experience as an immigrant.

CMarie Fuhrman authored *Salmon Weather: Writing from the Land of No Return, Camped Beneath the Dam: Poems* and co-edited *Cascadia Field Guide: Art, Ecology, and Poetry*, and *Native Voices: Indigenous Poetry, Craft, and Conversations*. Publications include *Terrain.org, Emergence Magazine, The Ex-Puritan, Northwest Review, Yellow Medicine Review, Poetry Northwest*, and *Inlander*. CMarie directs the Elk River Writers Workshop, and is Associate Director of the Graduate Program in Creative Writing at Western Colorado University. www.CMarieFuhrman.com

Jessica Gigot is a poet, farmer, and writing coach. She lives on a small, sheep farm in the Skagit Valley. Her second book of poems, *Feeding Hour* (Wandering Aengus Press, 2020) won a Nautilus Award and was a finalist for the 2021 Washington State Book Award. Jessica's writing and reviews appear in several publications such as *Orion, Taproot, Terrain. org, Gastronomica*, and *Poetry Northwest* and she is currently a poetry editor for *The Hopper*. Her memoir is *A Little Bit of Land* (Oregon State University Press, 2022).

Roger William Gilman is Professor of the Philosophy of Biology and a Poet who has been poetry editor of the *Chicago Review* and of *Adventures Northwest*. He is a mountain climber and fly fisherman. He has worked for NATO in Europe and been an Academic Dean of a college, has worked on a variety of restoration biology projects, and has published philosophy, science, and poetry. In retirement he teaches Theories of How Metaphors Make Their Meaning for writers at the Hugo House literary center in Seattle. roger.gilman@wwu.edu

Author and biologist **Thor Hanson** is a Guggenheim Fellow, a Switzer Environmental Fellow, and winner of the John Burroughs Medal. His books include *Close to Home, Buzz, Feathers*, and *Star and the Maestro*. Thor's work has been translated into a dozen languages and earned many accolades, including the Phi Beta Kappa Award in Science and three Pacific Northwest Book Awards. He co-hosted the PBS series *American Spring Live*, and has appeared on programs ranging from *Fresh Air* to *Science Friday*, and WIRED *Currents*.

Inés Hernández-Ávila, Niimiipuu/Nez Perce and Tejana, is a poet, scholar, visual artist, language worker, and Professor Emérita in Native American Studies, UC Davis. She is enrolled with the Colville Confederated Tribes. She is a member of *Luk'upsíimey/The North Star Collective*, a Nez Perce creative writers group working on language revitalization. Her book, *Indigenous Poetics*, co-edited with Molly McGlennen (Ojibwe), Professor at Vassar, will be out in April 2025 from Michigan State University Press, American Indian Series.

Ann Batchelor Hursey's poems have appeared on Seattle buses, in *the Seattle Review, Raven Chronicles*, and *Crab Creek Review*, among others. She collaborates with a variety of artists, and has authored poems to compost and hand-made-things. Ann authored *A Certain Hold* (Finishing Line Press, 2014) and her hybrid poetry/prose book, *FIELD NOTES to Maya Lin's Confluence Project* (Salmonberry Press, 2022). She speaks for oak prairies, salt marshes, and riparian restoration. Her poems celebrate the resilience of our planet.

Linea Jantz, among other adventures, has taught Business English in Ukraine (pre-invasion), worked as a bike law paralegal, and helped film a short documentary about women entrepreneurs in the state of Chiapas, Mexico. Her writing is featured in publications including *Palette Poetry, Heavy Feather Review, Beaver Magazine*, and *EcoTheo Review*. She has been a presenter for the Poetry Moment for Spokane Public Radio and volunteers in her community supporting youth writers. www.lineajantz.com

DJ Lee is a Pacific Northwest writer, scholar, and artist. Currently a Regents Professor of English at Washington State University in Pullman, her creative writing includes over forty lyrical essays and prose poems in magazines and anthologies; her memoir is *Remote: Finding Home in the Bitterroots* (Oregon State 2020). She has also published eight scholarly books on wilderness, 19th-century literature, and oral history. www.debbiejlee.com

Carolyn Maddux, a retired newspaper reporter/editor, lives in Shelton on the southwest Salish Sea. She teaches creative writing, and has two books of local history, two of poetry, and a murder mystery in print. She volunteers with Hypatia-in-the-Woods, a nonprofit offering residencies for women in the arts and academia, serves on committees for salmon restoration and climate resilience, and plants camas and redwoods on a piece of rural creekside property

Jill McCabe Johnson is the author of three poetry books and two chapbooks, and editor of three anthologies. Her most recent book, *Tangled in Vow & Beseech*, was a finalist for the Wheelbarrow Books Poetry Award and MoonPath Press' Sally Albiso Poetry Award. Jill is the founder and editor-in-chief of Wandering Aengus Press. When not writing or editing, Jill can be found exploring the nearest trail. jillmccabejohnson.com

Jeanne Morel is the author of three chapbooks, I *See My Way to Some Partial Results* (Ravenna Press), *Jackpot* (Bottlecap Press), and *That Crossing Is Not Automatic* (Tarpaulin Sky Press). She lives in Seattle and writes about other places.

Harriet Morgan is the Climate Change Coordinator for Washington Department of Fish and Wildlife (WDFW). In close collaboration with internal and external partners, Harriet is working to facilitate the development and implementation of a coordinated agency response to the impacts of climate change at WDFW. Before joining the agency, Harriet worked as a Research Scientist at the University of Washington Climate Impacts Group (CIG) for seven years, where she was involved in many facets of climate resiliency across the region—from planning to implementation.

Sky M. Pagaling is a poet from the Kalispel Indian Reservation. Drawing from his cultural roots, his work reflects the beauty and challenges of contemporary Indigenous life. Published in *Snilitn: Writings About Home*, Sky is a featured poet at the 2022 *One Heart Intertribal Poetry Slam* who has coordinated seven Native American events for Spokane Expo '74. A community leader and advocate for Indigenous entrepreneurship, Sky aims to inspire future generations to embrace love, leadership, and empowerment while honoring their heritage.

Victoria Pinheiro brings her background as a fisheries ecologist and her enduring reverence for nature to her creative work, which often centers on themes of impermanence and connectivity. She is the author of *Neighbors*, a limited-edition handmade chapbook designed and produced by Tori Haynes of Common Area Maintenance Studio (2024). Her work has also appeared in *Pomeroy Street Poets* (Honeybee Press, 2016).

Joseph Powell has published seven collections of poetry. The two most recent are *Holding Nothing Back* (Main Street Rag, 2019) and *The Slow Subtraction: ALS* (MoonPath Press, 2019). A new collection is forthcoming from MoonPath press called *Motion Against Our Moorings*. For his poetry he won an NEA in 2009. He grew up near L.T. Murray land and taught in the English department CWU for thirty years.

Rena Priest is an enrolled member of the Lhaq'temish (Lummi) Nation, and served as Washington State Poet Laureate (2021-2023). She has earned numerous awards and fellowships. Her debut collection, *Patriarchy Blues*, received an American Book Award and *Sublime Subliminal* was published as the finalist for the Floating Bridge Press Chapbook Award. *Northwest Know-How: Beaches*, includes 29 beloved Pacific Northwest beaches. Her nonfiction has appeared in *High Country News*, *YES! Magazine*, *Seattle Met*, and elsewhere. She holds an MFA from Sarah Lawrence College.

Linda Russo is a poet, writer, and student of ecospheric care. Their most recent book is *the verdant*, co-winner of Middle Creek Publishing's Halcyon Poetry Prize. She co-edited *Counter-Desecration: A Glossary for Writing Within the Anthropocene* (Wesleyan University Press) and *Geopoetics in Practice* (Routledge). You can read their poems online at *Chant de la Sirène*, *Ecotone Magazine*, *Interim*, *Plumwood Mountain Journal* and *Quarterly West*. She teaches at Washington State University and directs *www.EcoartsonthePalouse.com*.

Lindsay Senechal is the Lands Data Liaison for the Washington Department of Fish and Wildlife (WDFW), where she coordinates data management efforts to support and tell the story of WDFW-managed lands statewide. Prior to WDFW, Lindsay worked with Cal Fire, researching greenhouse gas impacts from forest fuel treatments, and also held a role at California State Parks, helping manage and preserve historical collections through research, documentation, and artifact care.

Derek Sheffield is a long-time resident of North Central Washington. You can usually find him teaching English and Nature Writing at Wenatchee Valley College, sauntering through pine trees and sagebrush, or editing poetry for *Terrain.org*. He received a 2024 Pacific Northwest Booksellers Award for *Cascadia Field Guide: Art, Ecology, Poetry*. His other collections include *Not for Luck*, *Through the Second Skin*, and *Dear America*.

Misty Shipman is a member of the Shoalwater Bay Indian Tribe. She holds a BA in English Literature with a minor in professional writing, an MFA in Creative Writing, and a PhD in Native American Literature and Film Studies. A member of the Spokane Poetry Slam's 2018 Nationals team, she competed in the Individual World Poetry Slam in 2017, and performed on Spokane's Grand Slam finals stage two years in a row. She has been writing poetry since age 6.

Scot Siegel is a city planner, educator, and author of four full-length books of poetry, most recently, *Tender Currencies* (2025), winner of the Sally Albiso Book Award from Concrete Wolf-MoonPath Press, and *The Constellation of Extinct Stars and Other Poems* (2016) from Salmon Poetry. Siegel has received fellowship residencies through Oregon State University, and Playa at Summer Lake, among others. www.scotsiegel.com

About NatureCulture® Web

The mission of NatureCulture® is to help humans be in right relationship with the rest of the natural world. NatureCulture Web is our new imprint for books brought to us by like-minded authors and organizations.

Please see all NatureCulture's publications at:
https://www.nature-culture.net

Other NatureCulture® Books

2025

Dark Matter: Women Witnessing, Dreams Before Extinction, eds. Weil, et al
The Nemo Poems: A Martian Perspective, by Rodger Martin
The Sleeping Dogs of Lubec, by Rodger Martin
Writing the Land: Rensselaer County, NY Hoosic River, poems by David Crews

Writing the Land: Streamlines Migrations and Home: The Elements of Place, ed. Simon Wilson
From Root to Seed: Black, Brown, and Indigenous Poets Write the Northeast, ed. Samaa Abdurraqib

2024

The Black River: Death Poems ed. Deirdre Pulgram-Arthen
Cayman Brac From Bluff to Sea
Writing the Land: The Connecticut River
Writing the Land: Wanderings I
Writing the Land: Wanderings II
Writing the Land: Virginia
Wriring the Land: Maine II, A Gathering
Writing the Land: Northeast

2022

Writing the Land: Foodways and Social Justice
Writing the Land: Windblown I
Writing the Land: Windblown II
Writing the Land: Maine
LandTrust, poems by Katherine Hagopian Berry

Forthcoming (2025-2027)

Writing the Land: The Cayman Islands
Writing the Land: Pathways
Writing the Land: The Great Forest of Aughty
Turning Poems into Food: A Collection of Poetry X Hunger Poems, ed. Hiram Larew
Handfast, poems by Katherine Hagopian Berry

2023

Writing the Land: Youth Write the Land
Writing the Land: Currents
Writing the Land: Channels

www.ingramcontent.com/pod-product-compliance
Lightning Source LLC
Chambersburg PA
CBHW051146120626

46547CB00012B/963